Practical Short Story Writing

JOHN PAXTON SHERIFF

ROBERT HALE · LONDON

© *John Paxton Sheriff 1995*
First published in Great Britain 1995

ISBN 0 7090 5547 1

Robert Hale Limited
Clerkenwell House
Clerkenwell Green
London EC1R 0HT

2   4   6   8   10   9   7   5   3   1

Photoset in Times by
Derek Doyle & Associates, Mold, Clwyd.
Printed in Great Britain by
St Edmundsbury Press Ltd, Bury St Edmunds, Suffolk.
Bound by WBC Book Manufacturers Limited,
Bridgend, Mid-Glamorgan.

Contents

Dedicated to my wife Patricia
for her patience and encouragement

Introduction

They say that if you don't know what to write about, then you have no business being a writer.

That obviously makes sense if you hope to become a full-time professional churning out x number of words each and every day. But if you want to write the occasional short story and already enjoy putting words on paper, then it's quite natural to want to know how to proceed: how to find useable ideas, and what to do with them to transform them from a hazy mental image into a short story that stands a good chance of being published.

So when planning this book, I used as a starting point the problems I had when I first began writing some thirty-five years ago, and the solutions I would have appreciated at that time.

It is, above all else, a practical book, presenting not a mishmash of daunting literary theories that aren't of much help when you actually sit down to write, but several basic rules that will enable you to produce a technically sound short story.

Already I'm probably treading on sensitive toes, because 'basic rules' and 'technically sound' are terms that might be used in building construction, but are usually frowned upon in literary circles.

Yet, surely, those are just what most beginners need to get started; and once started – and experiencing the sheer delight that comes from reading through their first, completed work of fiction – then the way is clear to experiment, and to go on to develop individual fiction-writing styles that will satisfy those who treat rules and regulations with disdain.

I was twenty-two when I sat down with a Parker Slimfold to pen my first story. The idea I had was of a gamekeeper entering a moonlit clearing in the woods – but because I had no idea what to do with it, that's exactly how it remained.

This book passes on to you the knowledge that has come to me through many years of browsing through books on how to write, and – I'm sure – thousands of hours of laborious though totally absorbing trial and error. Back in 1960 a gamekeeper entered a clearing with a furrowed brow and a number of obstacles to overcome. If I were to set him in motion again now, I know he would go on to a satisfactory resolution of his still unfinished story.

My earnest hope is that you can change a few words in that penultimate sentence – substituting 'writer' for 'gamekeeper' and 'book' for 'clearing' – and several pleasurable weeks or months from now sit back with a contented sigh knowing you have achieved the same, exhilarating result.

I've said nothing about talent. Yes, I firmly believe that to reach publication standard you must have a spark inside you, a natural feel for words that cannot be taught. But you cannot know if you have that spark until you are able to put a complete short story down on paper....

1 Thoughts on Short Story Writing

The vast majority of people who decide they would like to write begin with a short story. Often there is no conscious decision. They start with a vague idea that seems suitable for development, settle down with pen and paper, and the result usually turns out to be a satisfactory tale of between, say, 500 and 3,000 words in length.

Inexperience is one reason why few beginners start with a novel. The idea they set out with is usually simple; once their main characters have done what they set out to do, there is nowhere else to go and so the story ends. With experience a writer might worry at the basic idea, poking it around on the page until it begins to flow in different directions. Each tributary will lead to a fresh complication, and with enough complications what began as a short story idea can soon become the core of a novel.

Another reason for producing a short story is because what I call 'inner space' is strictly limited. By that I mean that the conscious part of the brain is like a box of a certain size. In that one box – the 'work box' – we can store and view an entire short story. A novel, on the other hand, must be stored in several boxes, only one of which we can look into. We can see Chapter 1 because it will be in our 'work box'; but because of limited 'inner space', it must be taken out and replaced by another as we look at each of the chapters in turn.

And then there's impatience. A short-short can be finished in a couple of hours, a longer short story in two or three days. This reasonably manageable working time appeals to the new writer, whereas the time required for the successful completion of a novel – anything up to a couple of years – cannot be contemplated.

According to the pundits, however, all those beginners are wrong. A novel is easier to write, they say. To begin by trying to write a short story is to start the hard way: the choice involves a literary form that requires great economy of writing and skilful construction, both of which are beyond the capabilities of the beginner.

Well, my own view is that the very term 'beginner' suggests someone for whom all writing techniques will be difficult: novel, screenplay, stage play – or short story. And if there is a burning desire to write – no matter what the odds – then it's far quicker to write six short stories, each one better than the last, than to serve your apprenticeship labouring over the same number of novels but taking twelve long years to do it!

You will have your own views on that, I'm sure. But by choosing to read this book you have already shown more than a passing interest in the short story, and to help you decide which direction your writing should take we will look in this first chapter at:

- Your personal approach to the short story
- The various forms of short story
- Opportunities in the various genres
- Formula, or originality
- Marketing, agents, income
- Writers' circles

Your Personal Approach to the Short Story

There's something ... unusual ... about writing fiction.

With painting or sculpture there's no problem. You nip into a field and splash watercolours on cold-pressed paper or oil on canvas, and you've captured a particular view. Or you take a slippery chunk of clay, mould it this way and that way, and what you have to show people (besides dirty fingernails) is a recognizable shape – perhaps the family cat. If you turn out to have no talent, that's the end of it. Your other secrets are preserved.

But all fiction writing is personal, even intimate. Until we start writing, nobody (we believe) can look into our minds. Yet once we decide we're going to write fiction, what ends up on the paper in our typewriter or printer is not a picture of a herd of Friesian cows under an oak tree or Tiddles cat-napping – but our private, innermost thoughts. This is a form of exposure. A lot of people are loath even to admit that they write fiction. Others make the admission – meekly, as if expecting ridicule – but refuse to let anyone read their work.

This is perfectly normal. And having established that, let's clear away those shimmering ghouls of impending embarrassment by saying that if you want to write entirely for your own pleasure, that's your affair. There is supreme satisfaction in seeing words appear on paper exactly as they were formed in your mind – indeed, if there wasn't, few people would bother with what is extremely hard work. And if you are looking for a hobby to while away the long winter evenings, nothing makes time pass more quickly than the pleasurable work involved in writing a short story.

However, even the most die-hard of closet writers will, in time, want a second opinion. It's always difficult to view your own work objectively, and the route many writers choose when seeking an objective opinion is to submit their work to one of the many short story competitions. These are held regularly by writers' magazines such as *Writers News* and *Writers' Monthly*. *Woman's Own* holds an annual competition, and the rewards for winners can be substantial – certainly far more than an unknown writer could hope to receive for magazine publication.

Nevertheless, most beginners who persevere with their writing will, ultimately, seek that wider audience that can only come through publication in a national magazine. And this is when the game really begins, for from the moment you send your first story away with an SAE for its return, you are living with a dream. How close you get to achieving that dream – whether it's publication in a magazine read by millions, winning a competition, or satisfaction with writing for its own sake – can to a certain extend depend on the type of short story you decide to write. Some will come easily. Others will, for you, be difficult. And the field is enormous.

The Various Forms of Short Story

It's been said that if you set out to write a book, the sensible thing to do is to look first at the type of book you normally read. Meaning that if you are an avid reader of thrillers, you are unlikely to be comfortable writing a Mills and Boon romance.

I'm not so sure the same reasoning can be applied to the short story. If you read short stories, you probably have fairly catholic tastes, picking up what you can, where you can, and generally devouring everything from short, twist-in-the-tail mysteries on the back pages of *Best*, to mini-novelettes in the more literary publications.

But you will have your favourite field, or genre. And if we are going to put short stories into their respective pigeon-holes, the result will turn out something like this:

CRIME
Under this heading I've jumbled everything from the traditional British detective/mystery story to the hard-boiled detective story which began, legend has it, when real-life Pinkerton detective Dashiell Hammett first put pen to paper.

The father of the detective story is said to be Edgar Allan Poe, who began it all in 1841 with *The Murders in the Rue Morgue.*

Any discussion of the British mystery inevitably involves

both novels and short stories. The general consensus is that this eternally popular literary form was born with the publication, in 1868, of *The Moonstone*, by Wilkie Collins – but that was a full-length book. Move forward twenty years and, with the appearance of Sherlock Holmes in *A Study in Scarlet*, Arthur Conan Doyle was creating an unforgettable character who trod his idiosyncratic way through both books and short stories. Most people would say he had greater success with the latter.

Other writers wrote books featuring popular characters and went on to success similar to that enjoyed by Conan Doyle, which is surely a salutary lesson: create a memorable character and you will kindle in even the most ordinary of stories that vital spark of life.

Names of great character-creators that spring to mind are E.W. Hornung (Raffles), G.K. Chesterton (Father Brown), Sapper (Bull-dog Drummond), Rex Stout (Nero Wolfe), Ross Macdonald (Lew Archer), and John D. Macdonald (Travis Magee) – the list goes on and on, and of course includes writers of novels and short stories from both the traditional and the hard-boiled schools....

In the traditional English mystery, women writers are pre-eminent. Beginning with Agatha Christie in 1920, we can trace a long and successful line through Dorothy L. Sayers, Margery Allingham, Ngaio Marsh and, in more recent times, P.D. James and Ruth Rendell. The first two named created memorable characters in the grand tradition – Hercule Poirot, Miss Marple, Lord Peter Wimsey – while Ruth Rendell, although the creator of Chief Inspector Wexford, tends to drift away from the fairly rigid structure of the traditional detective story.

In essence, this very English story form begins with the discovery of a body, after which a detective (often amateur, but with notable exceptions such as Dalgleish, Morse and Wexford) follows a number of false trails littered with red herrings before trapping the murderer by means of his/her incredible powers of deduction. The police are often made to look foolish, and frequently stand by looking shamefaced/ furious as the clever sleuth reveals all to a spellbound/ terrified audience in the library or billiards room.

The American hard-boiled detective story bears a great many similarities, but the methods differ. One of its exponents, Raymond Chandler, is often quoted as saying, 'If you don't know what to write about, have a man come through the door with a gun' – and that accurately sums up the style.

Between the traditional English and the hard-boiled American there is an infinite number of styles and settings. These range from the popular Maigret stories produced by Georges Simenon, the charming Inspector Ghote stories of H.R.F. Keating (usually short novels), to the impressive series of 'police procedurals' of Ed McBain (book length).

It's just occurred to me that I seem to have spent a lot of time talking about crime in one form or another. I make no apology, however, because now that the shelves in our libraries have been reorganized into categories rather than authors, the crime section is the one where you need to use your elbows.

SCIENCE FICTION, FANTASY AND HORROR
I was brought up on a diet of science fiction and fantasy stories because my father had a relative in the USA who regularly sent parcels of *Amazing Stories, Weird Stories*, and *Astounding Science Fiction* (*Black Mask*, too, incidentally, so I also soaked up a lot of hard-boiled detective yarns).

That was back in the 1950s, and among the names regularly being published were Frederick Pohl, Robert Heinlein, Henry Kutter, Theodore Sturgeon, Ray Bradbury, and many, many more.

The line between science fiction and fantasy/horror was quite clearly drawn. Science fiction looked into the future, with well-educated writes extrapolating to produce scenarios of life as they imagined it would be 10, 20 or 2000 years ahead.

Fantasy was imaginative without suggesting that anything in the story could actually happen. Indeed, much of it was set in the past, or in worlds peopled by wizards and goblins and strange mythical creatures.

Horror was blood and gore, enormous octopuses rising from the deep to overwhelm ocean liners, the living dead prowling dark city streets. But there were also horrific works of art by the masters of this genre – Edgar Allan Poe, Ambrose Bierce, H.P. Lovecraft, and many more including Daphne du Maurier and Robert Louis Stevenson.

ROMANCE

This is another of the special sections now found in most libraries, and although it has very few short story collections, I'm mentioning it because as a short story writer you will be looking seriously at the women's magazines – and that usually means romance.

HUMOUR

The funniest British short stories – in my opinion – came from the pen of P.G. Wodehouse. He was quintessentially English, as is Richard Gordon or Tom Sharpe. For counterparts across the Atlantic one need look no further than Damon Runyon, James Thurber and – in more recent times – Woody Allen.

The problem with written or any other kind of humour, of course, is that it seems simple – but isn't. Unlike a gory murder, which is almost certain to shock most people, humour is so individual that what makes one reader chuckle out loud will leave another totally unmoved. But because it's so difficult to do well, it's always in demand.

LITERARY

Now, what does that mean?

If we were talking about full-length books, then I'd suggest that if it didn't fit into any of the above categories, it must be 'literary': something likely to be found on the annual Booker short-list. And the same sort of yardstick can be used for the shorter work. But in long or short works, the line is a little blurred. A story has to be about something, so you'll find literary stories about crime, about romance, about the supernatural – about anything at all. The difference is in the way they're written, and there will be much more of that later....

Opportunities in the Various Genres

Before we take a closer look at the market-place, let me digress somewhat and explain my own approach to getting published.

Many of you will have read that the way to get into print is to take published stories from the magazine you are hoping to sell to, and – metaphorically – tear them to shreds. With those tattered remnants in front of you, you must then study everything: length of words, sentences and paragraphs; mood; types of hero and heroine; language – coarse, refined, modern, old-fashioned; and you must then devise a plot and produce a story that matches all those criteria. If you don't follow that advice – you are told – then you have no hope of selling your work.

I have never done that.

As you work through this book you will learn how to produce stories that, in their construction, are as near perfect as you can get. But they will be your stories, from your ideas. The most I would recommend as far as market study goes is for you to discover which magazines publish women's stories, which publish men's, the likely age of the readership and whether they are *Times* or *Sun* people. And I'm convinced that's all you need to know.

With that out of the way, let's now concentrate on the opportunities available.

Those in the know say that the short story is making a revival, yet for the writer sitting back with a satisfied sigh as the paper-clip is slipped onto a finished story, the hard part is still to come. A stroll along the shelves of any newsagent will reveal an enormous number of magazines, but the sad fact is that if we ignore the women's magazines, *The Telegraph* seems to be the only one publishing short stories.

Now, that doesn't mean there are none around. It just means that they're not on the newsagents' shelves, either because the market for them is virtually non-existent, or they are published in another country. But if we leave those elusive publications for a moment and concentrate on the ubiquitous women's magazines, what opportunities are there for those writers who specialize in genre fiction?

Of course, the writer of romances is in luck. Most women's magazines take at least one romantic short story, some take two. But *Woman and Home* looks for originality, *Woman's Weekly* does the same and doesn't specify romance (other than in its serials), while *Bella* and *Best* will also take crime or mystery stories, usually short and with a twist in the tale.

Several of the women's magazines in the USA look for very high quality, and the competition there is intense. Some won't countenance overseas locations. At least one won't even reply unless you have made a sale. The reverse side of the coin is that pay can be excellent: some mention $1000 as a start, others pay even more.

Once we move away from the women's magazines, then we need to scratch beneath an apparently barren surface.

There are one or two science fiction monthlies in the UK, but apart from *Interzone*, they tend to come and go. Fantasy is more likely to find a market, because its boundaries are blurred and it can well drift into the literary field and sell to such publications as *Panurge, Sunk Island Review* and *Granta*. Horror is always difficult to place, though if it's not overly gory it might find a home with publications that accept supernatural tales.

The USA has a far wider selection of SF and fantasy magazines. They include the old *Analog Science Fiction* and *Amazing Stories*, plus *Isaac Asimov's Science Fiction*

Magazine and several others with small circulations that pay no more than $5 per story.

At the time of writing there is no magazine in the UK equivalent to the *Alfred Hitchcock Mystery Magazine* or *Ellery Queen's Mystery Magazine*, both published in the USA. They are devoted to crime fiction in all its many guises; *Ellery Queen*'s maximum length is 6,000 words, while *Alfred Hitchcock* will look at stories up to 14,000 words in length. Both take stories from the UK, and are willing to look at new writers. An average fee for a 3,000 word story would be about £120.

Granta has already been mentioned as an outlet for literary stories, and others in the UK include the *London Magazine* and the *Literary Review*. The USA has several – *The Atlantic Monthly, Esquire, The New Yorker* – while in Canada *The Malahat Review* buys up to twenty manuscripts each year. There are many more 'little' publications in the USA; they take short stories, but often pay in copies of the magazine.

Humour will always sell. And the beauty of it is that humour has its place in all the other genres.

Study of the two premier books for writers – *The Writers' and Artists' Yearbook* and *The Writer's Handbook* – will reveal many more possible homes for your stories. The D.C. Thomson group takes general and family stories and publishes the *My Weekly Story Library*, Ireland has opportunities for stories with a local setting, and you will find magazines in Australia, New Zealand and South Africa so that your list of possible markets will, with perseverance, be quite long. Very widespread, too; but a sale is a sale whether it's in Dundee or Durban, and there's something splendid about the notion of becoming an 'international author'.

Formula, or Originality

I've mentioned formula when discussing the acceptable level of market research at the beginning of this chapter: when you study published stories you are looking for something that makes a particular story absolutely right for a particular magazine; a formula for success. An extreme example of formula is a Mills and Boon romantic novel, written according to the rules laid down by that publisher. And if you do delve as deeply into published short stories as many experts suggest, then I suppose what you unearth will – in some cases – be a formula: the writer has assiduously studied the target magazine, selected certain elements common to each story, and as if painting by numbers has then constructed a story that should sell because those common elements are incorporated.

You already know my views on this. If there's one thing that should come across to you as you read this book it's that you must write for yourself. By all means write a crime story, a romantic story, or a story that has the editor falling off his chair laughing. And when you have written your story, be sure you send it to a magazine that publishes crime stories, or romantic stories, or funny stories.

But once you get beyond the framework, if you start to ape what others have written you are seriously jeopardizing your chances of success. Copying a story obviously won't work. And if you are still struggling to find your own style, how can you possibly hope to write well in a style that belongs to someone else – or to nobody at all, but is merely a style that dubious research suggests will find editorial favour?

As you progress with your writing you will find that at times each and every word comes with difficulty, at others your mind is a spring from which flows an unending stream of fluent narrative and natural dialogue. Common sense will tell you that the writing that issues so freely from the subconscious is more likely to be good writing, and anything written to a formula must be done with conscious effort, and is likely to be bad.

Yes, of course that's an over-simplification. There will be times when each word you write brings sweat to your brow, yet the result will be magical prose. But if you need proof that chasing writing success by sticking to a formula is like using a Ouija board to find out if it's raining when all you need do is look out of the window, then select from those familiar magazines the stories that really catch your imagination. You will find that the element common to them all is not the number of words to a sentence, the colour of the hero's hair, or the 'girl meet boys, girl loses boy, girl regains boy' formula – but originality.

And if you can discover within you that rare spark – you will sell.

Marketing, Agents, Income

Much of the above is applicable to a marketing strategy, for marketing after all is the art of putting the right goods in front of the right people, at the right time.

From all that we've discussed above you will now be preparing yourself to write an original story that fits into one of the various genres – without being a slavish imitation of any one style – which will be sent to a magazine that either specializes in that genre, or will look at any original story of quality.

What you must not do is put your story away in a bottom drawer (but see Chapter 9) because you are too timid to do anything else with it.

Ridiculous? Far from it. In an earlier paragraph I mentioned that some people are loath to admit that they write. They fear ridicule, and putting a story before the experienced, critical gaze of a magazine editor invites outright rejection, usually without comment. Yet anyone hoping to sell their work must overcome this perfectly natural shying away from exposure, and put each story in front of editor after editor until it sells, or they run out of markets.

There is no easy route to success.

You may have read that employing the services of an agent will give your work an edge, but the sad fact is that few agents will work with new writers, and those that do rarely handle short stories anyway. Agents make their living by way of the commission they receive, and it's quite clear that – for a busy agent – the effort needed to sell a short story far exceeds the reward.

For the price of two manila envelopes and a stamp for outward and return postage, you can put your own story on an editor's desk. The editor behind the desk must be one likely to be interested in your work, and there are several ways of selecting the right one.

The cheapest way is to join the crowds browsing through the magazines on a newsagent's shelves. Many of the glossy publications will already be known to you. Some you may buy each week or month. For the rest, it takes but a few minutes to pick up a magazine and glance at the contents page. If fiction is listed, you can get the overall feel of the story or serial by rapidly scanning the pages (remember, I don't recommend deep analysis). In this way you will compile a list of some half-dozen magazines – mostly for women – and have their addresses and a brief description of the style required jotted down in your notebook.

This kind of market research will always need to be done, because you will want to keep abreast of the new magazines that are launched almost every month.

MARKET NEWS

But as a writer seriously setting out to be published, you will want to have before you at your desk one or two reference books that list hundreds of publications, many of which won't appear in your local shop. The two such books already mentioned are *The Writers' and Artists' Yearbook*, and *The Writer's Handbook*. The latter gives detailed coverage of the magazines it lists, but all the information is on UK publications. *The Writers' and Artists' Yearbook* on the other hand gives less information about individual magazines, but does cover Africa, Australia, Canada, Northern Ireland and the Republic, New Zealand and South Africa.

I am a great admirer of American writing, and am delighted to have broken into that market. If you want to do the same then you must get your hands on the *Writer's Market*, an immense tome published by Writer's Digest books in Cincinnati. Like its British counterparts this covers almost every kind of writing imaginable, and includes several short chapters giving advice and encouragement.

The two British handbooks can be bought from good newsagents, or direct from the publishers. The American *Writer's Market* must be bought from Writer's Digest (you will find a list of useful addresses in the Appendix), or from the UK agents, Freelance Press Services.

Freelance Press Services also produce a mimeographed publication called *Freelance Market News*, which comes out eleven times a year. Both new and existing publications are listed, and as well as the valuable market notes – and an overseas section – there are comprehensive details of competitions.

Writers' Monthly is a glossy magazine with pages devoted to article writing, poetry, plays – and short stories. There are regular profiles of top writers, instructional articles, and a four-page market section that keeps you abreast of what editors are looking for.

A more recent publication of the same kind is *Writers News*. Published in Scotland, this gives similar information in a snappier form. Both also hold regular competitions, and considerable sums of money can be won.

INCOME

While most aspiring writers will be overjoyed merely to see their work in print, a cheque popping through the letter-box is always a welcome bonus. The 'little' publications in the USA that pay their writers in copies of the magazine are doing a worthy job of presenting good writing to their subscribers and giving authors a springboard from which to launch a literary career. But once beyond that stage, an author will expect a more substantial reward.

You will find as you leaf through the marketing magazines that some publications will quote a certain fee per thousand words, while others will state that payment is 'negotiable'. And there will be enormous variations. *Sunk Island Review* offers £10 per 1000 words; *Bella*'s payments vary, but are around £300 per 1000 words (though possibly not for short stories). And a move into the American men's market could bring as much as $2000 for one story sold to *Playboy*, or up to $5000 for a sale to *Esquire*.

Success brings increasing rewards, for you will be paid more for the second or third story you sell to a magazine.

Writers' Circles

It's been said that a writer leads a lonely life, but unless you are writing full-time, that problem shouldn't occur. However, you will find that you have little chance to talk about your work with others of a similar inclination; I've already said that many budding writers are loath to broadcast what they do in their spare time, and so getting them to come out of the woodwork can be a difficult task.

Those that do emerge, blinking, into the light of day, often find their way to a local writers' circle, and here they will find men and women from all walks of life (mainly women) – and a range of activities that can be of some benefit, or utterly useless.

The main purpose of a writers' circle is to provide a forum within which members' work can be read out, and discussed. I was going to say 'criticized', but that implies the presence of someone qualified to judge a story's worth. Most writers' circles are simply gatherings of beginners who, if not exactly massaging each other's egos, offer criticism which is rarely constructive, and which at worst can be damaging.

Nevertheless, my own doubts about the value of writers' circles should not put you off. I went to one when I was already a full-time writer, and was astounded to find that most members never submitted their work to editors. But for all the fine people there, that fortnightly meeting with other writers was a spur that kept them going; a reassurance that they weren't, after all, peculiar creatures who scratched away with quill pens while the rest of the world was earning a living.

And many writers' circles do hold competitions, do have among their members published authors keen to pass on the benefits of their experience – and do have regular guest speakers who, for a few short hours, bring to those aspiring writers a touch of that heady world that each knows is always, achingly within reach.

2   Ideas

I had my idea – that poor gamekeeper who, for all I know, is still wandering aimlessly about the moonlit clearing – and you will have yours, either clear in your mind or shimmering a little as it strives to take shape. And it's possible that with that idea and the methods expounded in Chapter 3 you might be able to construct the bare bones of a short story.

The simplest – and most unreliable – way of arriving at story ideas is called inspiration. Writers never stop working, and although they may be reclining in an easy chair with their eyes closed, their minds are continually unravelling (and ravelling!) tangled plots. Ideas flash through the mind in rapid succession, some complete, some half-formed; but unless there is a way of recording them they will just as quickly fade away, and be gone forever.

So for those flashes of inspiration, do get a notebook, and have it by you at all times. And, yes, that includes keeping it by your bed, for with ideas churning away in the subconscious the night hours can be particularly productive.

But you will note that in the first paragraph I used the words 'possible', and 'might'. That was deliberate, because I firmly believe that an idea itself must be absolutely right before it can be further developed. And so in this chapter we will not only look at several ways (in addition to inspiration) of finding ideas, but how to ensure those ideas are suitable for development – if necessary by beating each one into shape.

In this chapter we will look at:

- Three conflicts, three laws
- From a word to an idea
- Word association
- Expanding a theme
- Inversion
- Ideas from pictures
- All in the day's work
- The thirty-six dramatic situations

Three Conflicts, Three Laws

All ideas will not necessarily make good, saleable short stories. However, most ideas can be developed into the right idea for a story by the application of three principles which, for want of a better name, can be called the three laws of fiction writing. The first of these laws is:

1   All stories must tell of a STRUGGLE, or CONFLICT

If you write a story in which there is no struggle taking place, your characters will simply wander aimlessly across the pages, doing nothing of importance, heading nowhere. If you talk about a woman getting up in the morning, seeing her children safely off to school, spending a perfectly peaceful day during which nothing extraordinary happens and then retiring to bed tired, but happy, you have certainly told a story but that vital element is missing. Your readers won't be interested, because there is no STRUGGLE, no CONFLICT.

That sounds straightforward enough until we look a little closer at those two words, STRUGGLE, and CONFLICT. What exactly do they mean in fiction-writing terms? Well, once again there are three principles to guide us, because over the years it has been discovered that there are just three different kinds of struggle or conflict, and they cover every story ever written, or ever likely to be written. They are:

1   MAN AGAINST MAN: A poacher striving to escape from

a pursuing gamekeeper
2 MAN AGAINST CIRCUMSTANCES, OR NATURE: A woman unable to finish her washing because the electricity supply has failed
3 MAN AGAINST SELF: A man struggling to achieve success in business, but held back by character defects such as lack or confidence, or a fiery temper

It might be helpful if you read over the last few paragraphs to make sure you understand that important first law, and the three basic conflicts. Then write down one or two of your own ideas, using what you have learned. Throw away all non-struggle, non-conflict ideas that keep sneaking in. Show little boys struggling to save puppies stranded on narrow ledges, young girls torn between respect for their parents and love for the young delinquent, strangers fighting to claw a foothold in a foreign land.

MAKE YOUR IDEAS HIT SOMEBODY – HARD
You probably managed to come up with a number of good, workable ideas. Just knowing and understanding the first law and the three basic conflicts will have demonstrated to you that the right idea isn't all that difficult to come by. But now let's sharpen it up a little. We've got to grab the reader's attention, and really hold onto it, so let's elaborate on those simple conflict examples by applying the second and third of those fiction-writing laws. They are:

2 ALL conflicts must be of VITAL IMPORTANCE to the characters involved
3 The CONSEQUENCES OF FAILURE in their struggle must be DISASTROUS

Right, now let's see how those two additional laws can help. You've already met the poacher crashing through the woods with two pheasants in his hands and the gamekeeper breathing down his neck. That situation is certainly a conflict

(Man against Man) – but as it stands it's just a workable idea, not a story. So let's apply the second law, and see what we get.

> A poacher runs through a dark wood, pursued by a gamekeeper. He is no ordinary poacher. He has broken into the manor, and now holds papers to prove that he is the rightful heir to the estate. If he can escape, his whole life will change.

No, I'm not cheating. He really is a poacher, it's just that on this trip he was after a different kind of game. And this juggling with characters is something you will find yourself doing constantly as you bash ideas into shape. Anyway, whatever he is he's still running away from the gamekeeper – only now the whole atmosphere of the chase has been altered. Those papers the fugitive holds can make him a rich man. Suddenly, the struggle has become of VITAL IMPORTANCE.

Can it be left there? There's no reason why not, but the application of law number three will neatly tie up the situation.

> Our poacher has already been caught twice, and warned by the magistrates. Now he's done a bit of breaking-and-entering. If he is caught it will mean prison, hardship for his wife and child, and very little hope of proving his identity without those vital papers (which are certain to be destroyed, or hidden away).

Far fetched? Possibly – but as an example it serves its purpose. Let's go over it:

> The poacher trying to get away from the gamekeeper was the basic struggle or conflict (Law One).

> The fact that he had papers to prove his birthright made the struggle of vital importance (Law Two).

Because capture would mean the loss of everything, a spell in prison and hardship for his family, failure in his struggle would be disastrous (Law Three).

If you feel that what you've read so far is quite clear, go back to examples 2 and 3 given with the basic conflicts, and see if you can apply laws two and three. What is so important that the woman must finish her washing? What is driving the man on, and what will happen if he fails to achieve his ambition?

Easy, isn't it. But – yes, there's always a but – a word of warning before we go on. In their efforts to build up conflicts and make things generally catastrophic for their characters, novice writers often end up with stories where people are forever battling with man-eating sharks or hanging over cliffs by their fingernails, and that isn't quite what we're after. It's important to remember that everyday conflicts are important to ordinary people. For example, the problem facing a young mother who is delayed when driving to collect her young son from kindergarten is as vitally important – to her – as hitting an iceberg would be to a yachtsman sailing the Southern Ocean.

SUMMARY
The three Laws of Fiction Writing:

1   All Stories must tell of a struggle or conflict
2   All conflicts must be of vital importance to the characters
3   The consequences of failure must be disastrous

The three Basic Conflicts:

1   Man against man
2   Man against circumstances, or nature
3   Man against self

Finally to close this section on how to make sure your ideas are absolutely right, an example incorporating the idea of a mother delayed when driving to collect her son:

A STORY MUST EMBODY A STRUGGLE (Law One): A woman is delayed on her way to collect her young son from kindergarten.

THE STRUGGLE MUST BE OF VITAL IMPORTANCE (Law Two): She has recently been in hospital. Since her return, her son has been clinging to her, afraid to let her out of his sight. She has managed to coax him into kindergarten. If she fails to arrive to collect him, his hard-won confidence will be shattered.

THE CONSEQUENCES OF FAILURE MUST BE DISASTROUS (Law Three): Her husband is struggling to make a success of his one-man business. At the moment the situation is critical, and she needs to earn a wage to help him. She is starting a part-time job the following week. If her son will not stay at kindergarten, she cannot take the job. If she cannot work, her husband's business will fail.

And it really is as simple as that.

From a Word to an Idea

Sitting in an easy chair with your eyes closed while waiting for inspiration is all fine and dandy, but if inspiration stubbornly refuses to cough up, then something must be done. And you'll be delighted to learn that all you need is one word, and you're on your way. One word – and a little bit of stimulating work.

It goes like this. Take:

1 A word
2 A character
3 One of the three basic conflicts

Let's imagine that the first word that comes into your head is SNOW. We know that children like snow, so let's add a LITTLE GIRL. You've already learned that a story must contain a struggle, or conflict, so to complete your idea you must associate SNOW, and a LITTLE GIRL, with one of the three basic conflicts. We'll try all three in turn.

1 MAN AGAINST MAN: A little girl is building a snowman, at dusk. She glances into the house next door and sees a murder being committed. But her parents don't believe her when she tells them (how can she convince them?)

2 MAN AGAINST CIRCUMSTANCES: When building a snowman, a little girl throws a snowball and sees it smash the window of the house next door. She goes back into her own house, owns up, but neither she nor her parents realize that the breaking window has disturbed a burglar. Her carelessness has prevented a robbery. Other neighbours saw what happened, and the little girl is rewarded.

3 MAN AGAINST SELF: A little girl building a snowman picks up some stones for eyes. They sparkle. She takes them to her father, who realizes they are precious stones, probably from a recent jewel robbery. (He is a poor man. Should he tell the police, or sell the stones?)

Once this stage has been reached, you are ready to apply laws two and three to the ideas you have created from that single word, SNOW. In other words, once you have the little girl witnessing the murder you must make it vitally important that she convinces her parents, and must ensure that the consequences of her failing to do so will be disastrous.

One obvious way to heighten the tension is for the criminal to have seen the little girl as she threw the snowball, realize that she has seen (and recognized) him, and have him set out to silence her.

Word Association

This method was often used in schools. (Or it used to be

when I was there!) It can produce ideas by the score.

Several unrelated words are jotted down. These can be anything at all: nouns, adjectives, prepositions, verbs – it really doesn't matter. It does help to remember your market, the magazines you hope will take your completed story. For example, words with a feminine association should be chosen if you are looking for ideas for the women's magazines, and words with a definite masculine flavour for the action thriller. But don't be too rigid; keep reminding yourself that an original story will sell anywhere, and that nowadays, distinctions can be blurred.

Let's try CHURCH. We'll write that down, then follow it with KNIFE, then RUNNING and LIES, and finally SAILOR. (I really am making these up as I go along.) A motley collection indeed: CHURCH, KNIFE, RUNNING, LIES, and SAILOR. But once you have your list, these can be built on. For example, we could say a boy RUNNING through a CHURCH finds a KNIFE. Or, a boy RUNNING through a CHURCH-yard finds a KNIFE, then has to LIE when a SAILOR grabs him.

Now, something a little more elaborate:

1   A young boy in CHURCH with his mother. He glances along the pew. A man is sitting at the end. He is not wearing a jacket. The tattoo of an anchor peeps from beneath his half-rolled shirt sleeve. (SAILOR?) Against the man's body, beneath his shirt, the boy sees the outline of a KNIFE. The minister is in the middle of his sermon. At that moment the man jumps to his feet. 'LIES' he bellows, and he runs (RUNNING) from the church....

The birth of an idea. The beginnings of a short story, perhaps told from the viewpoint of a young boy as a minor character, starting when he gets his first glimpse of the violent Jed Cotrell....

2   A young girl walking in the rain sees a KNIFE lying in the gutter. She picks it up, turns it in her hands. While she is studying it a man RUNS up to her. He is dressed in the

uniform of a merchant navy (SAILOR) officer. He wears no cap, his wet hair is plastered to his forehead. He grips her arm fiercely. 'Whatever they tell you about me, don't believe them (LIES)....' He breaks off, casts a panic-stricken glance over his shoulder, and leaves her. She watches him RUN wildly across the road into a tiny, run-down mission hall (CHURCH). She has never seen him before....

By now you're probably way ahead of me and about to say, 'Hang on a minute, there's something missing from both those ideas!' And you're right. Law number one states that there must be a struggle or conflict, and so far there isn't one in either of those little cameos. And I must admit it's a deliberate omission. I want you to see if you can apply law one to both those ideas (remember how we elaborated on the 'poacher' idea), and then go even further and apply laws two and three.

Expanding a Theme

Behind the events unfolding in most published stories there will be a well-known moral, or theme – even if the author was unaware of it when sitting down to write. CRIME NEVER PAYS is one theme in particular that is in constant use, and is often mandatory in crime stories; some editors insist that the criminal must never be seen to be getting away with the crime.

The list is long, and there may even be some you have made up yourself to instil good behaviour in your children. But whatever they are and wherever they come from, a theme – properly expanded – can be developed into a story that will have the ring of truth.

Arriving at a short story idea by expanding a theme again begins by thinking of a character, and associating that character with that theme. CHARITY BEGINS AT HOME, for example, could lead to an emotive story featuring a woman who, bored and frustrated in her middle years, turns to social work helping the old and the lonely – blind to the fact that her own mother, who lives with her, could have helped fill the void. The painful truth is brought poignantly home to her when her mother, unaware that her daughter works there, arrives at the social centre seeking help because she, too, is lonely....

A BIRD IN THE HAND ... could be developed into the story of a man who stays in his relatively low-paid job while his friends are rushing to join a get-rich-quick scheme. This idea could be developed in several different directions. The employer could value the young man's loyalty and raise his salary (thus enabling him to pay for his wife's operation – remember, there must be a vitally important problem), while the hasty friends come to grief. Or the story could be deeper, the friends finding wealth and a measure of happiness, but at the expense of their integrity; are they really as well off as the young man who stayed behind? Perhaps the employer dies, and the young man is rewarded in his will, or takes over the business....

You've probably noticed that two of the themes I've used are actually proverbs. This is a very rich field. I have *Everyman's Dictionary of Quotations and Proverbs* in front of me now, and the list of proverbs alone takes up almost 100 closely printed pages. Random selections offer: A BULLY IS ALWAYS A COWARD; BETTER WED AT THE MIXEN (dung heap) THAN OVER THE MOOR (meaning choose a partner from near to home); and BETTER BE STUNG BY A NETTLE THAN PRICKED BY A ROSE (meaning it's better to be wronged by an enemy than by a friend).

The same book offers several quotations from the Bible, and these, too, can be used in the same way. BE SURE YOUR SIN WILL FIND YOU OUT; OUT OF THE MOUTHS OF BABES AND SUCKLINGS; HE THAT MAKETH HASTE TO BE RICH SHALL NOT BE INNOCENT; and, IF A HOUSE BE DIVIDED AGAINST ITSELF, THAT HOUSE CANNOT STAND, can all be examined for their various meanings and expanded by the introduction of an interesting character, one of the three basic conflicts, and the application of the three laws.

Inversion

If TWO WRONGS DON'T MAKE A RIGHT – as the saying goes – try working on an idea using the inversion: TWO WRONGS *DO* MAKE A RIGHT. How about a burglar who breaks into the same house twice. The house belongs to a police constable, who is ready for him the second time. The RIGHT comes into it when the constable is promoted after the timely arrest.

HONESTY IS *NOT* THE BEST POLICY leads to the story of a man who sees the son of his prison governor friend committing a crime, but decides not to say anything (even when questioned) because he believes the boy to be basically an honest and honourable lad. His faith is justified. The wrong is righted, and some time later, over drinks, the governor remarks that although he is a firm believer in the prison system, he shudders to think of any son of his doing time.

Inversion can help in much the same way as using plots taken from stories written by other authors. Reading through a magazine story will enable you to determine the BASIC STORY LINE. Reduced to its simplest form, this story line is nothing more than the author's original idea sketched out in much the same way as the ideas we have already discussed. The story of the woman struggling to get to the kindergarten is a good example. Once you have determined the basic idea behind a published story, inverting it will create another, different story.

a   ORIGINAL STORY: A BOY wants to marry a GIRL. He cannot, because he is a MOTOR MECHANIC and she is the daughter of a HARLEY STREET SPECIALIST who will not agree to the marriage. However, the specialist's car breaks down when he is on his way to attend to a VIP (Very Important Patient!) Predictably, it is the young boy who arrives to repair it. The doctor changes his mind, the young boy is welcomed into the family.

b INVERSION: A young GIRL loves a BOY but knows she cannot marry him as she is a SHOP ASSISTANT and the boy's mother is a SNOB. However, when the mother is on her way to an important engagement with her husband, she tears her dress. Because of her position, the girl is able to get it repaired (or replaced) in the nick of time. The mother relents, and agrees to the marriage.

All the essential details reversed, and the result each time is a different story with the same basic theme.

Ideas From Pictures

Logically, this method of finding ideas should come directly after inspiration, because sitting in an easy chair with your eyes closed waiting for that elusive spark of inspiration is not too dissimilar to gazing at carefully selected pictures and letting the mind wander where it will.

Both methods make use of a dream-like state; the difference is that when seeking ideas from pictures you actually have something before you to work on.

The first requirement is, of course, a supply of pictures. So get yourself some old magazines or newspapers and snip out any photographs that catch your eye. Their subject doesn't matter; literally anything will do. Once you have your pictures, there are two ways of proceeding.

The first method might be termed armchair plotting, and no writing is required until the ideas have crystallized and are ready for your notebook. For this approach, crowd scenes are particularly useful though, again, any interesting picture will do. Just settle back in your armchair, with your picture, and as you gaze at it let your mind wander.

The results might be something like this:

During her Jubilee year, I saw a picture of the Queen

surrounded by well-wishers, and among all the happy, smiling faces, there was one that wore an expression of sadness. It belonged to an elderly woman. At that point, sensing a story, I let my mind drift. Why was she sad? Had she once enjoyed the limelight, perhaps been a ballet dancer adored by the crowds until she was struck by tragedy? Or was she remembering pictures she had seen of the Queen's tours of Australia, the country to which her own husband had fled, years before, leaving her penniless? Where was he now? (You see, with something to get our teeth into we have moved out of the picture.) Had he gone downhill, ending up drifting with the human flotsam on the streets of Sydney's King's Cross? Or had he really made good, amassed a fortune from stock in a nickel mine and moved south to marry a Melbourne socialite ...?

One of my own stories published in the *Australian Women's Weekly* was superbly illustrated by a staff artist. The subject of the story isn't important, but the painting across the first two pages showed a woman dressed in light tropical clothing using secateurs on some glorious hibiscus blooms. The garden around her was lush. In the background a skiff motored across blue waters backed by a smudge of purple hills.

Obviously I knew the original story. Yet as I looked at that picture I was able to gaze at the various elements and create a fresh story; more than one, in fact, for it was possible to concentrate on the woman, or on the person – unseen, unknown – who was sitting in that distant skiff.

The second method is to select any one of your pictures, but this time sit at your desk with it and write down everything you can about the scene depicted. This is an exercise in seeing, rather than looking, and it helps if you imagine you are trying to describe the scene to someone who hasn't seen it; to bring it vividly to life by means of a word picture.

For example, if there is a faded photograph of a Victorian basement, describe: *the old kettle's soot-encrusted sides, the battered lid that doesn't quite fit*. Then, after a while, allow your mind to wander, and speculate on what might have been. Using the kettle as a starting point you might wonder ... *if at some time it had fallen from the tilted hob, striking the brass fender and spilling water over the dull red tiles.* Further mental questioning could lead to ... *Did the kettle fall, or was there a blow struck? Is that a bloodstain, there, close to the wooden table?* And so, with the introduction, perhaps, of a chamber-maid with her hands raised, her face a mask of horror, followed by the application of the three laws in turn, you are well on your way to a good story idea.

All in the Day's Work

Sometimes, nothing works. Ideas won't come. You try one method and discard it, try another, still nothing. One possible way out of this situation is to sit down at your desk and write a factual account of all that went on that particular day: how you set out for work by walking to the station, the frustration you felt when you missed the train and knew you were going to be late – for the second time that week!

Nothing is more soul-destroying than a blank sheet of paper, and an equally blank mind. Nothing is more likely to banish ideas for good. Writing factually like this is a simple way of putting words onto that blank sheet of paper; and believe me, after the first few sentences your attention will be wandering away from that factual account you are typing (after all, you are a writer, looking for ideas, and you are beginning to understand the process) and you'll be remembering how happy that bus driver looked and wondering why.... *Was this his last day at work before going into business on his own account? Or was he quitting his job to set sail for the Bahamas, in the yacht he built in his back garden? (Now, there's a problem, he built it in his enclosed garden and cannot get it out ... he has to have it ready for charter within eight weeks, or the bank will foreclose on his mortgage and....)*

The Thirty-Six Dramatic Situations

Three basic conflicts cover every story ever likely to be written. That statement is in itself both gratifying and frustrating. For although it means that we can develop a story by dipping our pen into one of just three simmering pools of conflict – surely not a difficult task – it also means that within those three conflicts there must must be an infinite number of possible situations.

Or are there?

A man called Georges Polti set out to discover just how many, and it may surprise you to know that according to Monsieur Polti, there are not countless situations, but just thirty-six. He listed each one of them in a remarkable book that I heard about quite early on in my writing career, but was unable to lay my hands on until a couple of years ago.

When you read *The Thirty-Six Dramatic Situations* – first published in 1921 – it becomes obvious that, as with the three basic conflicts, each entry can lead to a multitude of permutations. Situation 24 is the 'Rivalry of a Superior and Inferior'. For that situation to exist there must be a Superior Rival, an Inferior Rival, and an Object, and the possibilities are endless.

For our purposes, the information contained in *The Thirty-Six Dramatic Situations* gives us yet another excellent way of arriving at story ideas. For example, using Situation 24 I could have arrived at the idea featuring the young mechanic that I sketched out in the INVERSION section, but with the addition of an inferior or superior rival adding to the complications and strengthening the story.

And if you combine two or more of the situations – for example adding Situation 17 ('Fatal Imprudence – the Imprudent, the Victim, or the Object Lost') to Situation 24, then you can see how the young mechanic in our story could see his Superior Rival lose the girl they both desired by some act of stupidity – or Fatal Imprudence.

SUMMARY

What this business of finding ideas amounts to, of course, is observation. A writer must be alert the whole time, observing characters and incidents and seeing the story that *might* lie behind each and every one. We can PICTURE PLOT from life just as we did from magazine photographs, using the same routine of question and answer to arrive at ideas. We can draw together characters and objects and incidents and combine them in living WORD ASSOCIATION.

Striking first lines can be dreamed up (I keep several sheets of them, for inspiration): *Behind her, on the stairs, a loose tread creaked....* Or, *She slipped into the bedroom and on that calm, windless evening the curtains stirred, and were still....*

It doesn't matter if they are never used again. Use them now by asking yourself questions and arriving at ideas, then discard that first line – if you must – and go on from there. Jot down unusual titles, and ask questions, then more questions. Wasn't it Kipling who said:

> I kept six honest serving-men
> (They taught me all I knew):
> Their names were What and Why and When
> And how and Where and Who

Draw on inspiration, by all means; but when that fails don't dry up. At that point, turn to the methods discussed in this chapter. Read your NOTEBOOKS, PICTURE PLOT and ASSOCIATE WORD groups and EXPAND THEME after theme; and when you've exhausted those possibilities you will still have TITLES, and STRIKING FIRST LINES and simple OBSERVATION to fall back on.

That's the key, of course. Observation. All the time.

3   Plotting – From Idea to Story Skeleton

In the last chapter we discussed several ways of finding good ideas for short stories, and it's now unlikely that you will ever approach that hated blank page without the faintest inkling of what to write.

The section on conflicts has already demonstrated that for an idea to be workable it must be developed into a situation which involves the interplay between two or more characters, between character and self, or between a character and circumstances (or nature). Merely by creating such basic situations your mind will have been stimulated; and if you imagined, say, a gentle circus clown who has been ordered to stand in for an injured lion-tamer – or that jealous sailor we met in Chapter 2 – you will already have explored several ways in which those situations could be developed.

Now it's time to learn how to create a plot from your original idea, but create it in such a way that when your story is written your readers are hypnotized from the outset, and literally compelled to read on in order to satisfy the curiosity your skilful story-telling has aroused.

For a beginner, the simple way to do this is by using a standard set of bare bones to create a consistently sound story skeleton. I am going to show you four headings – with a couple of sub-headings – which together with their instructions constitute the best method I have found for constructing a foolproof plot. If you like, you can think of this as a short story formula, although many people will be put off by that term. Throughout this book I'll refer to it by

the name under which I file it on my word processor –
PLOTSKEL. I use it, at least at the outset, for every story I
write.

In this chapter we will be looking at:
- Basic plotting
- Detailed plot construction
- Dramatic scenes
- Creating scenes to expand a draft plot

Basic Plotting

First, it might be a good idea to decide what we mean when
we talk about 'plot'. And to keep it very simple, I always
imagine a plot as a pathway through the dense woods of an
absorbing tale; an often wriggly line that sometimes doubles
back on itself but nevertheless traces the sequence of events
in any story. There are countless technical or literary ways of
defining it, but for me, that simple description says
everything.

Following on directly from the last chapter, at the moment
you will have nothing more than an idea for a story; a few
scribbled lines that delineate a character faced by an
apparently insoluble problem which must be tackled because
the outlook is black. Now that idea must be licked into
shape, complications added, and a satisfactory solution
arrived at – and any idea, no matter how hazy, can be
developed into a story by using the following PLOTSKEL.

Step by step, the stages are:

SITUATION

In which a character is in conflict with another character,
with self, or with circumstances.

Incident One

Something occurs, which increases or intensifies the
character's problems, and heightens the tension.

Incident Two

There is a second incident, perhaps arising from the first, which makes the character's predicament much worse.

REACTION

The character attempts to overcome the problems.

FRUSTRATION

The character's attempts are thwarted by the introduction of yet another complication, *which must be entirely different from the first two*, and which further intensifies the situation.

REACTION/RESOLUTION

The character again attempts to overcome the problems, and either succeeds – in which case the story comes to its conclusion – or is again thwarted, and there are second REACTION and FRUSTRATION stages leading to a final RESOLUTION.

This PLOTSKEL is nothing more than a device for creating a workable plot. But it is a practical device, and as such it can take you from being a writer with little more than a hazy idea to someone who has gone one step further; to someone who now has a sequence of events which – even at this basic level – are recognizable as a story.

Earlier in the chapter I used the example of a gentle clown who has been ordered to take the place of the lion-tamer. That is a typical situation of conflict (man against self – or is it man against man?), and if you wanted to proceed further – to create a plot to carry the clown's story – then you would begin by writing a brief statement of his predicament in the SITUATION stage of your PLOTSKEL:

SITUATION

A circus lion-tamer is injured. The ringmaster asks Slapdash the clown to take his place. Although terrified, Slapdash agrees.

You would then rack your brains to find two INCIDENTS that would make Slapdash's situation worse. Let's say that after much thought you decide that ordinary lion-taming is too easy. You arrange for one gentle old lion to die during the night, and have the circus boss bring in a strange lion, of unknown temperament. That's incident number one.

To complete the SITUATION stage you need one more incident that intensifies the conflict. Perhaps the clown trips over a bucket and sprains his wrist (now he will have difficulty cracking the whip, or holding the chair), or his wife threatens to leave him if he walks into the cage (putting him in the wrong frame of mind for tackling a strange lion).

Incident One

The lion-tamer's skills have been exaggerated because Fang, the lion he works with, is old, toothless and harmless. During the night, Fang dies. Determined not to cancel the show, the ringmaster decides to introduce a young, unpredictable lion that has never been worked.

Incident Two

Woken by the commotion, Slapdash falls out of his caravan bed and sprains his wrist – and discovers that his beautiful young wife has walked out on him.

Almost every short story ever written was created by placing a character in a situation of conflict and having that character react to overcome problems that appear overwhelming. If the story is a short one, it will consist – referring to the pile of bare bones I've dubbed the PLOTSKEL – of a SITUATION stage, a REACTION stage, a FRUSTRATION stage and a REACTION/RESOLUTION stage. Longer stories will have the basic SITUATION, two or more REACTION and FRUSTRATION stages following each other (in which none of the problems are resolved), and a final REACTION/ RESOLUTION stage in which the character wins through – or loses, depending on the mood of your story.

Detailed Plot Construction

If all of that, at first glance, is about as clear as someone whispering a foreign language in a dark room, then let's throw some light on the subject by using the PLOTSKEL to construct a simple plot. I've already started you thinking about our trembling clown who's going to tread the sawdust with an unknown lion, so I'll leave you to weave that web by devising suitable REACTION, FRUSTRATION and RESOL-UTION stages. But for the purpose of instruction I want to take a more detailed look at the story of the sailor with green eyes who even now is hurrying off the quay....

SITUATION

> A sailor working on oil tankers has always harboured (no pun!) the suspicion that his wife is not faithful to him. But he arrives home on shore-leave happy, and determined to put those suspicions out of his mind.

Incident One

> He immediately hears rumours that his wife is seeing another man.

Incident Two

> Determined to be fair, he sees his wife off on a visit to her sister, and goes to church. Unfortunately, the sermon is all about an unfaithful wife.

REACTION

> Not feeling confident enough to resolve the situation on his own, the sailor decides to talk to his brother – the one person he always turns to for help. He telephones him, learns that

he is busy that day, and arranges to meet him the following morning.

FRUSTRATION

He goes home, his mind more at ease. His wife is still out. The next door neighbour hands him a telegram. There is an emergency, and the sailor must return to his ship. He has been absent without leave once before, and dare not ignore the order.

REACTION/RESOLUTION

Desperate, he goes straight to his brother's house, and discovers why he was 'busy': his wife is there, not with her sister – and the sailor's own brother is the 'other man'. The sailor walks out, determined to forget his unfaithful wife and concentrate on his career.

That little plot is certainly not intended to be a model of sophistication. Yet even such a well-worn situation can be turned into a compelling story because we have developed the original idea – with the help of the PLOTSKEL – by adhering to story-telling principles that are as old as time.

Remember how, in Chapter 2, we talked about three essential elements that must be present in every story idea? There must be a struggle; that struggle must be of vital importance; and failure to overcome the problem must be disastrous. You will see that this little plot fulfils all of those requirements, and in the way it is set out it is ready to be developed into a chronological story; a classic tale in the tradition of 'Once upon a time....'

As far as the actual construction of the plot is concerned, note the two incidents that compound the sailor's problems. He is reasonably happy when he arrives home – after all, although he is suspicious, in his heart he is hoping that his marriage is still secure. Then he hears the rumours, and when he is trying hard to come to terms with that information he suddenly finds himself listening to a sermon – about an unfaithful wife.

Note, too, that in the instructions for the FRUSTRATION stage, I pointed out that the additional complication must be completely different from previous complications. And so in the basic plot we have constructed, the sailor is at that stage faced with either having to return to his ship, or go absent without leave and ruin his career – a fresh dilemma.

You'll notice that a couple of paragraphs back I mentioned that in its present form this is a simple, chronological story. In fact that would only hold true if we were to follow our intrepid sailor's adventures without changing the order of events – and that isn't always the best way to present your story.

But, I digress; you will learn more about the ways in which the elements of plot can be juggled in the next chapter. For the moment let's examine the plot we have created, with the headings removed.

A sailor is unsure of his wife's fidelity, but is determined to forget his suspicions. However, he has scarcely set foot on dry land before he hears rumours that seem to confirm his suspicions. When he has to sit through a sermon about an unfaithful wife, he is driven to act. But the course he takes is frustrated by his brother's busy afternoon, and when he receives a telegram ordering him back to his ship, he becomes desperate. His final, impulsive reaction is to go to his brother's flat. When he arrives there he discovers that his wife has not gone to visit her sister – and the only reason his brother is busy is because he is the 'other man'. The problem has been solved, perhaps not as the sailor would have wished, but certainly in a way that leaves him free to pursue his career.

We have come a long way from our first sight of Barnacle Bill in Chapter 2, and all we have to do now is to begin putting flesh on the bones. And the way to begin – the final stage before the actual writing of the story – is by creating a number of dramatic scenes, so that our hero's adventures are presented in a series of vividly-painted pictures that not only bring the story alive, but also carry out several other important, story-telling tasks.

Dramatic Scenes

What is a dramatic scene?

If you've watched television, or been to the cinema, then you already know part of the answer. Take a typical (imaginary) episode of *Only Fools and Horses*, by John Sullivan. It opens with Del and Rodney talking in their flat; moves to the pub where other characters are introduced; switches to Rodney and Cassandra in her car; and after a few more scenes, returns to the flat for the resolution.

If you're not familiar with this series, it doesn't matter. What I have described are various stage settings – a flat, a pub, a car – that could be part of any screen or stage play. Each one is a scene, and when we make something happen in these scenes – create conflict by the interplay between our characters – then we have a highly-charged, emotional situation: in other words, our 'dramatic scene'.

But, what is it that makes one scene tense, dramatic, totally absorbing – and another just one long series of yawns?

Let's look at a couple of examples.

Little Johnny is happily playing on the beach. Big waves are breaking on the sand. Each time the water recedes, Johnny runs onto the wet sand, waits for the next wave, then runs away as fast as he can. When one enormous wave rolls in, he is too slow. The wave knocks him off his feet. He gets up, and continues with his game.

That's one scene. Here's the second.

Little Johnny is on the beach. His mother is smiling, but telling him not to go near the water because the waves are dangerous. Johnny nods, and begins to play. After a while he notices his mother is fast asleep on her towel. He looks longingly at the big waves. Then he runs down to the water's edge, and begins to play another game. As each wave rolls in, and recedes, he runs onto the wet sand, waits for the next and runs away as fast as he can. He keeps glancing at his mother to see if she's still asleep.

As he waits for one very big wave, two boys run past, shouting and laughing. They carelessly drop a surf-board. Johnny doesn't see them. He has one eye on his mother, the other on the monster wave. It roars in, and he begins to run. Looking over his shoulder, he runs straight towards the surf-board. He trips over it. The big wave tosses him into the air and he disappears into the foam. His mother wakes up, screaming.

The same location. Almost the same scene. Both versions could be the same length, depending on how long you're prepared to have Johnny successfully racing the waves in the first scene. But it's important to note that in that first scene, nothing happens. Johnny runs. He gets drenched. He runs again. And that could go on for page after page as the reader yawned, then nodded off.

But what a difference in the second!

There is suspense. We hear Johnny's mother telling him the waves are dangerous, so we expect something to happen; we have been forewarned, and anticipate a dramatic event. Later, we see the boys approaching, and again we know something is going to happen – but we're not sure what. We *want* to read on; and as the drama unfolds, we are kept on tenterhooks. When the board is dropped, what is about to happen next becomes obvious, yet when Johnny trips and disappears under the boiling surf, we are still shocked. We will continue to read the story, because we want to discover the outcome.

There is one more important element in the make-up of a dramatic scene that may become obvious only when it's pointed out: almost always, there is an EMOTIONAL REVERSAL. For example, in the above scene, Johnny and his mother start by enjoying their day at the beach, but it ends in tragedy. And so it must go with every scene. Start happy, end sad. Or begin at a low point, and gradually build up to a joyful high. It needn't be quite as clear-cut as that, but in every scene you construct there should be some reversal, however slight.

To summarize, then, a dramatic scene should:

- Paint a vivid picture
- Create an air of anticipation
- Have emotional reversal
- Generate the urge to know what will happen next

Oh, and there's also something else that a scene often has – or doesn't have, depending on how you look at it – and that's the gap between one scene and the next. And that convenient gap is one of the ways a writer can move his story forward in time, and to a different location. The technical term is TRANSITION, and you will learn more about the technique in Chapter 5.

Creating Scenes to Expand a Draft Plot

Now, let's use what we've learned to begin putting flesh onto the skeleton of our Tale of the Jealous Tar.

Scene 1   A handsome sailor is leaning against the bar in his favourite, city-centre pub. He has just walked in out of the pouring rain, but he is happy because he is home on leave, and he is telling his friends how much he is looking forward to seeing his wife.

As he drinks his pint he asks them if they have seen much of her while he has been away. All of them seem reluctant to discuss her, merely mumbling their excuses, then moving away to play darts or pool.

The sailor thinks it very odd. Gradually, as he drinks, his mood darkens. He has already noticed

the barman casting glances in his direction. With a
sense of foreboding, the sailor calls him over and
asks what's going on. Reluctantly, the barman tells
him. There have been rumours. It seems the
sailor's wife has been seeing another man.

Notice how this dramatic scene, just like the second
featuring Johnny on the beach, has all the essential
elements. If you look back at the four points in the
summary, you'll find that all are included. The picture is
VIVID. ANTICIPATION gradually builds up as the sailor
begins to realize something is wrong. The EMOTIONAL
REVERSAL is very clear. And, of course, the reader wants to
know WHAT HAPPENS NEXT.

Now let's work through the remaining scenes.

Scene 2   Next morning the sailor walks into church and
greets acquaintances, choosing not to notice if
some glances slide uneasily away. He hears
nothing of the early part of the sermon. He is
thinking about the previous evening. He had gone
home, said nothing to his wife about the rumours,
and she in turn had acted normally. The evening
was enjoyable, and the sailor woke up in the
morning, elated. He is convinced everything is all
right, and the rumours were just malicious gossip.
Then, as he becomes aware of his present
surroundings, he begins to listen to the sermon. It
is about an unfaithful wife. As he listens, all his
fears come flooding back, and he runs from the
church.

Scene 3   The sailor is in a phone booth. He is distressed. He
keeps ringing the same number. The phone rings,
but there is no answer. Then his face lights up. His
brother has answered the phone. The sailor says he
must see him, and his face drops momentarily as
his brother tells him he is busy. But they arrange to
meet the next day, the brother reassuring him that

no matter what the problem is, they will resolve it. The sailor leaves the phone box, whistling.

Scene 4　He is walking up the path to his house, still whistling. A neighbour hands him a telegram, which he stuffs in his pocket. His brother has always helped him with his problems, there's no reason why this time should be any different. He puts the kettle on, and while he waits, gets out the telegram, reads it. He is stunned. He has been called back to his ship, and must leave at once. He knows he must go. He has been absent without leave before, and knows his career is in the balance. He looks up as the kettle whistles mournfully....

Scene 5　The sailor is ringing the bell to his brother's flat. The brother comes to the door, tries to close it, but the sailor pushes past. He sees his wife on the settee, half naked, and realizes the truth. He looks at his brother, goes to hit him, then thinks better of it and walks out. As he walks towards the docks, his shoulders square. He begins whistling again, but off key....

I'd like you to pay particular attention to the EMOTIONAL REVERSAL in each of those scenes, because if you examine the way each one progresses you will see that the reversals rarely have to be worked at – they occur naturally.

Let me explain. Take Scene 4. The sailor spoke to his brother in the preceding scene, and at the start of Scene 4 he is happy because he is looking forward to meeting him the next day, and resolving his problems. But we are at the FRUSTRATION stage of our basic plot, and according to the instructions something must happen – in this scene – to give the sailor another knock.

When it does – the arrival of the telegram – he is devastated.

It may help to look at this EMOTIONAL REVERSAL in

another way. If the sailor is happy at the beginning of the scene, and still happy at the end, then nothing has happened to arouse our interest. It's like a routine visit to the doctor. If my GP tells me I'm perfectly healthy, there is no story. But if he tells me I have some incurable tropical disease I picked up in the Amazon jungle....

To sum up: as writers, we must create incidents within scenes that will have a strong effect on the feelings of those characters involved. Because a good story is a tale of conflict, those incidents must have a dramatic effect, making the situation better, or much worse. As a result, characters become elated, or despondent – but they must never remain the same.

In this expanded skeleton or plot you'll notice that there is a scene for each of the intensifying incidents, and for the REACTION, FRUSTRATION and RESOLUTION stages. It's always possible to have more than one scene for a stage in the PLOTSKEL, or even to have two stages completed within one scene. But no matter how many scenes you create it's important to remember that in this chapter we have been looking closely at plot construction, and that the skeleton we build in this way will not only be hidden beneath the flesh of the story, it may also end up with some of its bones in strange places. In other words, for the purpose of drawing the reader into the story it may be taken apart, and assembled in a different form.

But that really does take us into the next chapter.

4   Technique – One

If you were to write our sailor's story exactly as it stands, it would be a straightforward chronological story, beginning with the onset of his problems and proceeding through a number of incidents until those problems were resolved. Nothing much wrong with that approach, and in many cases it will work reasonably well.

But we are not looking for something that will work 'reasonably well'. We want to create a story that will have the best possible chance of catching an editor's eye, and to do that we must not only choose exactly the right point in our tale to begin, we must also ensure that we include – very early in our story – elements (tricks, if you like) that over the years have been found to draw readers into a story.

In this chapter, then, we will be looking at:

- Where to begin – and why
- The beginning – the five essentials
- Viewpoint
- First or third person
- The use of language to establish mood

Where to Begin – And Why

In order to draw your reader into your story, you must begin at a dramatic high point. Usually, though not invariably, that's when your main character is at the REACTION stage.

One of my short stories was about an old man living in a

cottage at the foot of a Welsh mountain, who learns that there are plans to site a wind farm on the slopes. Knowing that the peace he has enjoyed all his life will be disturbed – first by the construction work involved, later by the wind turbines – he decides to put a herd of Jacob sheep on the slopes to deter the planners.

The story opens on a hot day in late summer when he is plodding up a lane to see his neighbour. He is reacting to his problem, and after a few brief, descriptive paragraphs, in the way he shouts at his neighbour's son on the way up the hill the reader becomes aware of his anger:

> One more example, Gwynfryn thought bitterly, listening to the fading percussion from the boy's earphones. Nothing against the young, mind, but give that lad five or six years and he'd be up from university drafting madcap schemes to drive old people from their homes.
>
> Like wind farms, aye!
>
> And as memories of why he was plodding up the steep hill to Eifion's farm came rushing back, irrational anger surged and he called wildly after the disappearing figure, 'Take your wind farm, boy, you hear me! No way you can farm the wind, it's time you're wasting on sheer bloody nonsense …!'
>
> And he was still muttering angrily five minutes later as his boots clattered on the stones of Eifion's yard and the young farmer's border collie, sprawled like a black and white rag in the sunlight, lazily twitched an ear in welcome.

But at that point the nature of the problem has not been revealed. Instead, it comes out, gradually, in the old man's conversation with his neighbour.

> 'I've gazed across Pen Cefyn for almost seventy years,' Gwynfryn said, his gnarled hand trembling a little as he clutched the glass of cold water. 'It would be wrong to see those ghostly shapes rising from gorse and heather....'
>
> 'Common land,' Eifion Williams said bluntly. 'Bordered by dry stone walls, rises nine hundred feet, all year round it catches the prevailing winds driving cold and pure from

Snowdon. Can surely be no finer place for a wind farm,
Gwyn.'

If we look at the basic plot of our sailor story (Detailed
Plot Construction in Chapter 3), there would seem to be two
possible starting points. In this case the REACTION stage is
probably a little too far into the story – too much will need to
be presented in flashback or through the sailor's thoughts. A
better place is Incident Two – itself a reaction with an
incident at its end.

Now, here's another PLOTSKEL:

Incident One

A newly-married girl is looking forward to life with her
husband, when he is taken ill and confined to bed with a
severe bout of flu.

Incident Two

The problem is intensified when her husband reminisces
about the wonderful mushrooms he used to eat when he was
a boy, fresh from the field. The only way to get them is by
going through Hangman's Spinney to Finnigan's Meadow –
and the spinney is said to be haunted by Finnigan's ghost.

REACTION

The girl decides to go after the mushrooms.

We'll leave it there, because the later stages are not
relevant. I decided to begin the story at the reaction stage,
and this is how it developed:

'Johnny,' Mary Anne Moynahan said, fluffing the pillow
behind her brand-new husband's dark, curly hair.
'Uh huh?'
'Johnny, can I get to Finnigan's Meadow without taking
the path through Hangman's Spinney?'

'Sure,' Johnny Moynahan said. His face was flushed, his eyes heavy-lidded beneath a damp brow. A pink paperchase of tissues trailed from his limp brown hand, across the bedspread, and disappeared into the carton on the bedside table.

'Sure,' he repeated. 'There's a pair of gum boots in the shed, and you'll find a compass tucked away in the old trunk. A bull-fighter's cape might come in handy, too....'

'Are you trying to tell me there is no way?' Mary Anne said.

Johnny grinned weakly. 'What would you be doing in Finnigan's Meadow, girl? Picking daisies, is it?'

'Did I say I was going there?' Mary Anne asked innocently, her heart thudding as his wild guess narrowly missed the truth.

'But....'

'Ah, be off with you Johnny Moynahan! I said nothing. That fever's making your head light....'

It was eleven at night. They'd been married on Sunday and this was Tuesday and Johnny had been in bed the whole two days. They hadn't planned a honeymoon, preferring....

By starting at the REACTION stage the reader is allowed to enter the story at the middle of a dramatic scene. Mary Anne is about to set out across a haunted spinney, late at night – and we don't know why. The last paragraph is the start of a flashback sequence that will enlighten the reader, and after that the story progresses chronologically as Mary Anne embarks on her search for fresh mushrooms and encounters various incidents along the way.

As you can see, starting off at the REACTION stage works well, and in most cases anything that came before that point can usually be presented to the reader in an uncomplicated flashback that takes up little space.

I'll use that little cameo to illustrate other points.

The Beginning – The Five Essentials

Within the first page or two of your story you should have

accomplished the following:

1   Introduced the main character
2   Hinted at the problem
3   Set the scene
4   Established the mood
5   Cast your narrative hook

The first four of these are blended smoothly into the narrative and dialogue so that you succeed in arousing your readers' interest and communicating necessary information to them without their being aware of it.

The fifth essential – the narrative hook – must stand out. It is designed to grab your readers' attention and hold it.

The story that was unfolding just a few paragraphs ago was called, not unsurprisingly, *Finnigan's Ghost*, and it will serve well to show how those five essentials can be incorporated in your story without damaging the narrative flow.

1   INTRODUCE THE MAIN CHARACTER
In *Finnigan's Ghost* the main character is introduced in the very first line:

> 'Johnny,' *Mary Anne Moynahan* said....

2   HINT AT THE PROBLEM
The *initial* problem is hinted at on line six:

> His face was flushed, his eyes heavy-lidded beneath a damp brow.

... and actually stated three lines from the end:

> They'd been married on Sunday and this was Tuesday, and Johnny had been in bed the whole two days ...

3   SET THE SCENE
The setting of that first scene and those to come later in the story are described or suggested in a number of ways in that

first page. Mary Anne is *fluffing the pillow*. A paperchase of tissues trails *across the bedspread*. Mary and Johnny refer to *Finnigan's Meadow, Hangman's Spinney*, and *picking daisies*.

All of these examples take the reader into a bedroom, and the choice of location names suggest the house is in the country. And, to go right back to the beginning of the story, the name Mary Anne Moynahan surely suggests that the story is set in Ireland!

4 ESTABLISH THE MOOD

It is a ghost story, but a happy ghost story. The mood comes across as light-hearted, a little old-fashioned, rural. Many examples can be selected: *a pink paperchase of tissues, camphorated oil*, again the *meadow* and the *spinney* and, of course, Johnny saying:

> 'Sure,' he repeated. 'There's a pair of gum boots in the shed, and you'll find a compass tucked away in the old cabin trunk. A bull-fighter's cape might come in handy, too ...'

5 INTRODUCE THE NARRATIVE HOOK

A narrative hook is something that so grabs the readers' attention that they are forced to read on to satisfy their curiosity: you have hooked them by some narrative or dialogue that has aroused their interest. One of the things you must aim for is a telling first sentence (remember, I suggested thinking up striking first lines when looking for ideas), and if you can make that first sentence the narrative hook – without straining for it – so much the better.

In *Finnigan's Ghost* the narrative hook – in my opinion – comes on line four:

> 'Johnny, can I get to Finnigan's Meadow without taking the path through Hangman's Spinney?'

The readers know the title of the story, *Finnigan's Ghost*. Now, right at the beginning, this young girl is asking if she can get to Finnigan's Meadow and avoid Hangman's

Spinney. Why? Is she frightened of the spinney? Is there something we don't know? And why does she want to make the trip anyway? The readers' interest is aroused. They want to read on, to find out what happens.

SUMMARY
Notice the way in which one piece of narrative or dialogue can contribute to more than one of the five essentials. The main character was introduced and subsequent scenes set in the very first sentence. There can also be more than one narrative hook. In line eighteen Mary Anne's heart thuds as Johnny's remark narrowly misses the truth. His guess had been that she was going to pick daisies. What is she going to pick, and why doesn't she want him to know?

Viewpoint

In order to bring your writing vividly to life, and to enable readers to take an active part in your story, you must provide a viewpoint character through whose eyes the drama unfolds. Ideally – in a short story – your readers will stay with that character, seeing the same sights, thinking the same thoughts, experiencing the same emotions. Done skilfully, the story becomes much more than mere words on paper; it becomes a living drama in which readers – because they are at one with the viewpoint character – become actively involved.

This is the ideal to be aimed for. The degree of reader identification and involvement is governed by your skill – and by your careful choice of viewpoint. The ones we will be discussing in this chapter are:

   a   Single major character
   b   Single minor character
   c   Ranconteur
   d   Omniscient

THE WRONG WAY

The following short passage is a parody of a valid form of viewpoint that should rarely be used in the short story:

> Conscious of Karen's eyes on him from across the patio, Bill shook off his towel, stepped to the end of the springboard and dived into the clear, ice-cold water. He kicked powerfully, feeling the trail of bubbles across his face as he exhaled.
>
> Watching him, Karen felt the old, familiar tingle of excitement as his slim, suntanned body arched, then slid beneath the surface.
>
> Acutely aware of Karen's thoughts, Jane frowned, and felt a hot surge of anger.
>
> From his stool at the bar, Dave saw the shadow cross her face, and grinned. Here we go again, he thought ruefully.

There is an immediate sense of something being wrong, a grasshopper feeling of never being with the same character long enough to get involved. I've already said that viewpoint enables the reader to identify with the main character – yet in that deliberately concocted parody of short fiction it is impossible to tell which is the leading character. In the space of twelve short lines the reader is whisked through the thoughts of four different characters.

A good rule to memorize is that *the only thoughts and emotions you can reveal, throughout your story, are those of the viewpoint character*. My illustrative passage has broken that cardinal rule.

a   SINGLE MAJOR CHARACTER

Let's take a closer look at our four characters. In order to choose a viewpoint character, let's decide that Bill is engaged to Jane, Karen is secretly in love with Bill but is too nice a girl to push Jane out of the way, and Dave – sitting at the bar – is Karen's brother.

One good rule-of-thumb you can use to decide on a viewpoint character is to ask yourself, *whose problem is it*?

In the above example I'd suggest that Jane, Bill and Dave are quite settled, whereas Karen is tormented by her secret love for Bill. So let's rewrite that passage, with Karen as the viewpoint character:

> Karen felt the old, familiar tingle of excitement as she watched Bill toss away his towel and dive into the sparkling water. She knew Dave was grinning at her from the bar, and out of the corner of her eye she saw the shadow of a frown cross Jane's face. She didn't care. All she ever cared about was Bill....

The same story, much of the same information, but this time everything is seen through the eyes of the viewpoint character. This time, you experience Karen's emotions, are aware of her thoughts. What you cannot know is that Bill was feeling a trail of bubbles across his face; that even before he dived into the pool he was conscious of Karen watching him. *You* couldn't know, because *Karen didn't know*. Similarly, although you saw, through Karen's eyes, the frown shadowing Jane's face, you knew nothing of the hot surge of anger she was experiencing. And although Karen saw Dave grinning, she (and therefore you, the reader), knew nothing of his rueful thoughts.

From the above you will have gathered that all Single Character viewpoints have the following limitations:

> All emotions, feelings or thoughts of non-viewpoint characters can only be revealed to the reader by the appearance, actions and dialogue of those characters *as seen and heard by the viewpoint character.*

So, to sum up: when you select as your viewpoint character the person around whose problem the story revolves, you are using Single Major Character viewpoint.

b SINGLE MINOR CHARACTER
Although it is usually most effective to use the character with the problem as your viewpoint character, some stories

call for different treatment. If, for example, the character you intend writing about is a hardened criminal, and his wife a slattern, then neither of those characters would be suitable for reader identification. In such a case it might be preferable to tell the story from an observer's point of view; that is, from the viewpoint of a minor character. If the couple had a young son, then the story could unfold before his eyes, and readers would find themselves caught between true identification, and the genuine interest of an observer.

To return to our well-worn passage, if you had decided to tell Karen's story through the eyes of her brother, it might have turned out something like this:

> Karen had tried hard, but it had been obvious all summer that she was living with a problem. There's not a lot you can hide from your own brother.
>
> It all came to a head that hot, August afternoon at the swimming pool. I'd slipped over to the bar for a drink, and I noticed Karen watching Bill as he went in off the springboard. She seemed completely unaware of Jane's flushed, angry face ...

The viewpoint has been changed, but the story is still about Karen's problems. It's also still a single character viewpoint, so those same limitations and restrictions apply. The difference now is that the emotional impact of the story has, to some extent, been reduced. The character with the problem is being watched, and the thoughts and emotions with which the reader will identify are those of the sympathetic observer – Karen's brother.

Oh, there will still be tension. A story told this way is often very effective, because as well as watching Karen battling with her problem, the reader is now able to feel the effect it has on – in this case – her own brother. And Dave will have strong feelings for his sister, just as the little boy would be deeply affected by the conflict between his criminal father and slatternly mother.

Of those two viewpoints, you will probably use Single

Major Character most of the time. There are two more I'll discuss here. One is somewhat outdated, the other is rarely used in the short story.

c RACONTEUR

This is the name given to a method of telling stories that has gone out of fashion. An old man can be telling a story to a group of children gathered round a campfire; or one of the members of a London club might be chatting to his cronies when suddenly he is reminded of a chap he once knew, *funny feller, killed his wife in the end....*

There is no reader identification, because the ranconteur is not a viewpoint character. He goes into his 'Once upon a time ...' tale and the reader becomes one of the listening group.

d OMNISCIENT

This is used in many novels. The reader is allowed to enter into the minds of most of the characters, often switching from one to another in rapid succession (as in the earlier 'Wrong Way' example). However, although there is certain to be some identification with all the characters, there should still be a main character with whom the readers spend most of their time.

There is a variation of this method that is a little more relaxed, and less confusing. In the passage I've been using as an example, Karen's viewpoint would be used until she and her brother returned home. When she retires to the kitchen to make coffee the viewpoint switches to Dave and stays with him when she returns. Later, Bill might call in for a drink, and when he leaves the reader might go with him as the viewpoint switches again.

Another variation is to change the viewpoint at the start of a new chapter. This is often used in thriller novels, jumping from 'goodies' to 'baddies'. In this way the reader knows what each side is planning, whereas the factions involved are in the dark. An element of dramatic irony is introduced, the readers waiting with bated breath to see if the hero falls into the trap that they, the readers, know awaits him.

As far as the vast majority of short stories are concerned, the Omniscient viewpoint, with all its variations, is best forgotten.

First or Third Person

It's been said many times that telling your story in the first person means instant identification for the reader. Many people also feel more comfortable writing this way. You write letters in the first person, so it's something you've been familiar with for most of your life. And it does away with constantly having to decide between using a name, or pronoun: you know, should you say 'Bill thought', or 'he thought'?

Example 'b' above (Single Minor Character) illustrates the way the first person is used. Example 'a' (Single Major Character) illustrates the third person, and you will notice that only minor alterations are required to turn the one into the other. It's always a matter of author's choice anyway, but whichever you use it's not graven in stone and – particularly if you use a word processor – you can soon change over if you are unhappy with your first choice.

The Use of Language to Establish Mood

Of all the five essentials that must somehow be scattered unobtrusively throughout the first few pages of a story, establishing the mood is the one that gives me the most pleasure. It's said that in writing there are wordsmiths and storytellers, and if I were asked, then I suppose I'd have to admit that I'm a wordsmith. Reluctantly, because often mediocre writing will be overlooked if there's a rattling good story. But, again, I digress....

To give you an idea of what I mean by establishing the mood, the following is an extract from the first page of one of my stories:

> They brought the sheriff and the procurator-fiscal over from mainland Scotland for the Serious Accident Enquiry, but it was mid-winter and blowing a gale and they stumbled over the step into that hastily prepared room in Tobermory still looking green and shaken from the ferry trip. And that just about set the pattern. There were a lot of disgruntled faces, and I drew some black looks, but I'd heard enough gossip to know why. It was unnecessary, they argued; legal procedure should be adhered to, right enough, but it had been an accident, so what the hell.
>
> So in that bare, cold room on the Isle of Mull, with its crude wooden benches and iron-legged tables, I listened with the sour taste of fury in my mouth as big, bearded Dougail Gaunt told them what they wanted to hear with soft words and a twisted tongue. And long, long before he'd finished I was outside, leaning into the wind as I stumped disgustedly towards my car through the salt spray whipping in from the harbour.

This surely, is no romance! In fact, the story's title is *Fifth Time Dead*, the idea came to me in the flash of a car's headlights (observation), and it was published in the *Alfred Hitchcock Mystery Magazine* in 1991.

It was a harsh story, set in a harsh environment, and in establishing the mood at the very beginning of page one you'll notice that I used such evocative words and phrases as *mid-winter, blowing a gale, hastily prepared room, disgruntled faces, black looks, bare, cold, iron-legged tables, leaning into the wind, salt spray whipping* ...

The next is a similar type of story, but this time I began with a line of dialogue:

> 'Archie? For Christ's sake, it's Archie bloody Yendle!'
> The voice was shrill, disbelieving. Like an unexpected slap it sent shock waves rippling across his scalp, knocking him

back on his heels so that for a moment he teetered in the sea
of exhaust fumes lapping the edge of the kerb.

Once again, the reader is expected to know – at once –
that this is going to be a mystery story, a thriller of some
kind. The line of dialogue itself grabs the attention (hook?),
and that startled voice is followed by words chosen to
increase the feeling of shock felt by the viewpoint character:
*shrill, unexpected slap, shock waves, knocking him back,
teetered ...*

With careful thought you will be able to arrive at words
that quickly create the mood you feel suits the story you
have in your mind. I feel instinctively that it would be wrong
to suggest you compile lists, labelling each one romance,
thriller, supernatural, and so on – although there's no
denying they would be handy to have in front of you. What
you will have, after a time, is several stories in which
different moods have successfully been created, and a glance
at relevant first pages when you come to write your next
romance or ghost story will soon establish the right mood in
your own mind.

Here's another opening:

> The sun beat down on the back yard of the white,
> chamfer-board house, the shadow from the tall palm tree
> falling as a dark patch around the base of the slender trunk.
> Even seen through sun-glasses the oil-stained concrete drive
> leading to the double garage was dazzling, the heat reflecting
> fiercely into Binky's face and burning through the rubber
> soles of his thongs.
> 'Think you can manage that, Col?' he asked.
> The short, dark-haired man grinned cheerfully. 'No
> sweat,' he said, trundling the battered red lawn-mower
> towards the garage's inviting shade. 'Half an hour, she'll be
> running sweet as a nut.'

As well as establishing a mood through the use of words
and phrases – *sun beat down, shadow from the tall palm,
sun-glasses, dazzling* – this example also shows how the

choice of names can influence the 'feel' of a story. The lazy, laconic way the second man speaks also tells the readers that they are in for a relaxing read, and indeed they are, for this story was about an elderly Queensland couple and the way they were able to help the dark-haired mechanic and his young son.

Another similar example comes from a story set in Mexico:

> The hot wind gusted through the open door of the shoe shop, bringing with it a drift of dust. The dust settled on the rough, board shelves, on the huaraches fashioned for the peasants, and on the shiny black boots brought in from Mexico City for the elegant feet of the caballeros. It settled in a grey, powdery film, missing nothing.
>
> In a moment, he will sneeze, José Gardena reasoned. Then his small hammer will stop tapping at the last, there will be a creak from his wooden stool, and without looking at him I will know that his eyes have turned towards that shelf high in the corner. And if I do not move....
>
> Miguel Cardenas sneezed explosively.
>
> José sighed. He stood up and grinned across at his father, seeing the familiar, moustachioed figure, gnarled hands poised, dark eyes staring almost absently across the room at the shoes, that single pair of quite ordinary shoes standing on their small shelf set apart from all the others.

So far I have been stressing the use of various evocative words and phrases to establish the mood of your story. But another way a mood is suggested – rather than spelled out – is in the pattern of your writing; the way it looks on the page, which is really the manner in which you feed your thoughts to the reader.

Put at its simplest, short sentences coming in rapid succession create an air of tension. Longer sentences slow down the pace, put the reader at rest, create an air of calm. You will use this knowledge throughout your story – shortening your sentences at action sequences or as the climax approaches, lengthening them as the tension relaxes –

because of course there are are swings of mood as your story unfolds. But the mood that is to predominate must be established at the outset, and in the early pages the judicious choice of words and phrases, the names you have chosen for your characters, and the pace of your story, will all tell your readers the type of story they have before them.

Finally in this section I'd like to show you a blend of narrative and dialogue from the middle of a story. A mood, once established, must generally be maintained throughout that story or the reader will feel cheated. This little snippet is from a story set in India. The mood is unmistakable, and the piece moves us neatly into the next section.

Long minutes crawled past. Ali Ambedkar seemed fascinated by the movement of the papers. The truck driver was becoming more enthralled by the mountains; he continued to stare in the general direction of Everest.

The sun was hot on Ranjit Singh's neck. He shuffled his feet awkwardly and wriggled his toes in the dust.

'Rajah is an elephant,' he volunteered, when the silence had grown painfully long.

'The older the elephant, the stronger its back. Very definitely.'

'An old elephant is like an old man. His limbs grow stiff. His joints creak.'

'It has been said that an elephant's worth is in direct proportion to its size.' Ali Ambedkar was smiling, as if at some private joke.

'It is also a fact that an elephant can be handed down from father to son, from generation to generation. It can be said that such an elephant would be without price.'

'Nevertheless. I am telling you that even an old, much loved elephant could be sold – to pay taxes!'

Ranjit Singh said nothing, allowing the warm dust to trickle between his toes.

5   Technique – Two

- Characterization
- Dialogue
- Motivation
- Flashback and transitions
- How to handle flashback
- Transition techniques
- Style

Characterization

If stories are about people, then bad characterization, perhaps more than anything else, can leave the reader with a feeling of having been let down.

Some people begin with a character. They concentrate on developing that character before anything else, believing that it is better to build a story around a memorable character than it is to invent a stiff, artificial character and force him or her to conform to the twists and turns of a complicated plot.

I look at it a little differently, without entirely disagreeing. Yes, your idea will contain a rather indistinct character; you will recall that when plotting from a single, random word, a character must come into the frame very early. But it's as the idea develops that your character will take on more form, developing with it. Sketching in the scenes will continue that development and, at that point, you can set your story skeleton to one side for a while and take a closer look at your characters.

If a character is to fit a story, he must – in the beginning – develop with it.

GENERAL CONSIDERATIONS

Once our idea has been developed into plot form and the scenes blocked in, before proceeding any further your main character must be known intimately, your minor characters lightly sketched.

I am all in favour of knowing much more about your main character than you are ever likely to need. Taking our jaunty sailor as an example, you should know where he was born, what school he went to, all of his past life up to the chronological beginning of the story – and that includes what his parents were like. You must know his likes and dislikes, his ambitions and frustrations, his mannerisms and peculiarities of speech. His appearance must be familiar to you. And from all this information you must be able to predict how he will react in different situations; you must know his *dominant character trait*.

Lesser characters should be invented with much less detail. If a man is a lawyer, and a girl is a model, the readers will have stereotypes they can draw on to create their mental image, and the application of the techniques to be discussed will bring even these shallow characters to life.

It has been said by some writers that their characters acquire a life of their own, take over the story, and become uncontrollable. I like to look at it as a sort of catch-22 situation: your characters must appear to manipulate their own lives, but they cannot do that unless they are manipulated by you. In other words, make them act according to the fully-formed character you have created by the depth of your invention, and your characters will, indeed, seem to march with autonomy across the pages of your story.

Characters may be modelled on people you know, or have met; observation will provide the raw material, and the judicious blending of traits from different people will result in the creation of a memorable character. Because of the restricted length of a short story, direct character description should be kept to a minimum. Appearance and characteristics should be revealed naturally as the story progresses. In other words, don't say 'Mr Gates-Pemberton was a snob'; instead, show that he is a snob by the way he acts and speaks as the story unfolds.

METHODS OF CHARACTER PRESENTATION

    a   Direct description
    b   Dominant character traits
    c   Appearance
    d   Dialogue
    e   Actions – movements and gestures
    f   Thoughts and emotions
    g   Surroundings

a   DIRECT DESCRIPTION

Direct description is simply you, the writer, describing a character. It is best illustrated by an example:

> Mrs Smith was plump, round and cheerful. She laughed easily, and when she did her whole body shook like an enormous, pink jelly.

To distinguish this direct description from description through a viewpoint character, here is the same passage seen through the eyes and thoughts of Joe:

> Joe liked Mrs Smith. Plump, round and cheerful, she laughed easily, and when she did her whole body shook like an enormous, pink jelly. She fascinated him; he couldn't take his eyes off her.

Although that short piece contains the same information, those four words at the beginning make all the difference. It is now Joe describing Mrs Smith – not the author.

In a short story, it's best to keep direct description to a minimum.

b DOMINANT CHARACTER TRAITS

On the whole, people fit within well defined character classifications. Though most people have several different characteristics, one is usually outstanding; we have all heard of the nosy woman down the road, the man who has never worked but who knows how to run the world, or the barrister who treats differences of opinion between his infant children as major court cases.

We can bring our characters to life by giving them a slightly exaggerated dominant character trait. It is helpful to remember that minor characters, who may appear only briefly, require greater exaggeration than your main character. If a man is a bully, he must bully in some way on almost every occasion that he appears. Let the braggart keep bragging, and have that annoying woman poking her nose into everybody's business.

Characters in various jobs can be given character traits generally associated with that occupation: a lawyer will be shrewd, a racetrack tout shifty, the professor eccentric and absent-minded.

Do not let your characters act in a way that contradicts their dominant character trait. Unless temporarily affected by strong emotional circumstances (see below), or unless you are writing about an incorrigible rogue who turns over a new leaf, all your characters must act in character – and even that rogue will do so until he changes.

c APPEARANCE

The frequent references to the remarkable nose of Cyrano de Bergerac serve as both a lesson and a warning: by all means give your characters limps, patches over one eye and sallow complexions – but don't overdo it! Instead, try to arrive at a physical feature or manner of dress that is unusual in that particular person. For example, a scar on the face of our familiar sailor would raise no eyebrows. The same scar on the face of the minister reading the lesson would be unusual, and would create a character of interest to the reader.

However, once again, be careful. If a minor character is given an appearance that is too unusual, the reader might be misled into believing it is somehow linked to the plot, and will feel cheated if it proves to be insignificant.

d DIALOGUE
This is dealt with in detail in the relevant section.

e ACTIONS – MOVEMENTS AND GESTURES
People move in different, characteristic ways. The way they move can be influenced by their nature, their state of health, age, occupation and mood. Verbs describing movement should be selected with care. An old man may clump, plod, shuffle; a child crawls, totters, toddles; a braggart struts and saunters; a tired person trudges, stumbles....

As well as moving from place to place, people make various gestures, many of them unconsciously, and from habit. They bite their nails, run fingers through their hair, cross their legs, tap their feet, blink rapidly, lick their lips, twitch, adjust their clothing, puff nervously on cigarettes, flick ash, toy with drinks, drum their fingers – very rarely, in fact, does anyone remain perfectly still. (This point has been made use of many times, with writers creating characters with strange, unblinking eyes ... *whose stillness was the very stillness of death....*)

f THOUGHTS AND EMOTIONS
Because of the technicalities of viewpoint, it is possible to reveal the thoughts of the viewpoint character, and no one else. The readers are, in a sense, inside the mind of this character, and because they have access to the character's thoughts they also have access to his emotions. If the writer is doing his job, readers will always know what the viewpoint character is thinking and feeling.

Emotions in non-viewpoint characters can be revealed through the viewpoint character's thoughts, and by the way those minor characters react to different situations – flushing, turning pale, wringing their hands, and so on. The type of emotion is usually clear from the context, and need not necessarily be stated. A man will turn pale for several reasons; if he has been insulted he is probably angry, whereas if he has been accosted by an armed bandit, it's safe to assume that he is afraid.

Your characters' emotions can affect their appearance and actions, and can lead to unpredictable behaviour that forces them to act out of character. For example, entreme fear can turn a timid woman into a tigress; an intense emotional experience can make a strong man cry. But these aberrations merely serve to emphasize their dominant character traits. We are shocked at the strong man's weeping, and marvel at the way the timid woman fights. But we are comforted and reassured by the knowledge that when the crises have passed, each will return to more characteristic behaviour.

g   SURROUNDINGS

People can be characterized by their surroundings – a form of stereotyping. Recognizable types hang around pool-halls, spend their lives at the racetrack, become village constables or live in remote mountain villages beneath the towering Himalayas.

The Chinchilla Line was set in Australia, and this was how the story's main characters – Doug and Jenny – came across the spot where Charlie and Queenie Malone lived:

> At a battered yellow mail-box nailed to a post they found the track, an overgrown incline that doubled back, winding its way down towards the old man's diggings. The descent was steep, and rocky. As the swaying Campavan reached level ground and rounded a stand of slender gums the side of a drab caravan could be seen wedged against a raw cliff face. Beyond, at the edge of thick timber, a stout shelter had been

constructed from peeled logs and canvas awnings. A dying
fire sent a thin plume of pale blue smoke drifting towards the
road, high above.

Nobody would expect a man in top hat and tails to emerge
from such a dwelling, and indeed, having already met
Charlie, neither Doug nor Jenny were surprised by
Queenie's appearance:

> She was sitting in a tattered canvas director's chair in the
> dappled shade beneath the gums, drinking from a tin mug.
> Her grey hair, pulled into a bunch and tied, hung down in
> front of one plump shoulder. Her breasts were fat pillows
> beneath the broad pink sheet of her cotton blouse.
>   A gnarled stick was resting against her faded denim shorts.
> As the old man drew near with Jenny she leaned forward,
> planted the stick on the ground and climbed to her feet.

One final example, which has much to do with
surroundings but also presents Ranjit Singh (you have
already met him at the end of Chapter 4) to the reader in a
number of ways:

> He pushed open the door, and stepped into the warmth of his
> home. Just over the threshold he stopped, and surveyed the
> circle of faces that had turned towards his entry like flowers
> towards the sun. He let his glance wash over them. Anna,
> sitting with eyes downcast. Mrs Singh, her hands as always
> folded in her lap. Sang and Song, inseparable, their faces
> round and solemn, their shining eyes betraying the effort
> needed to remain serious for even a moment.
>   And a stranger.
>   Ranjit Singh walked slowly, all the way into the room. He
> sat down, his back resting against the wall, apart from the
> group, yet dominating it.

Dialogue

If observation is the key when seeking ideas, then 'listening'
followed by the careful editing of everyday speech is the way
good written dialogue is achieved. The student writer must

be alert to every nuance of speech, must be aware of different dialects and realize that they are not just funny accents but familiar words strung together in a different way. Care must be taken that the dialogue used by your characters is not dated. We all tend to be locked in our own time warp, but the world moves on day by day, year by year, and there are few things in it as changeable as language.

Although this can cause problems if we are writing a modern story and don't make the effort to study the way today's young people express themselves (our TV and VCR are useful tools here), when writing a period piece the use of contemporary language can enable us to bring those times authentically to life.

If you intend to write crime stories, then you need some knowledge of the cant peculiar to the world of the criminal. This, too, is constantly changing, and can even differ between the various criminal elements. Young thugs, old lags and the suntan and gold bracelet brigade on the Costa del Crime will all talk in different ways, and if you write a story set in the USA then you must be meticulous in your research.

The importance of good dialogue is undeniable. There are people who actually skim rapidly through narrative, and only take an interest when they reach the 'conversation' parts of a story. Yet even they would be put off by dialogue that didn't ring true.

THE FUNCTIONS OF DIALOGUE

1   To provide information
2   To advance the story
3   To characterize
4   To convey emotions

Stories should always be a balanced mix of narrative and dialogue. But, what exactly do we mean by 'balanced'?

Concerning the amount of each, there cannot be – nor

should there be – any reliable guide. Some stories work well with virtually no dialogue. Others have been written with so much chatter they resemble the script for a stage play. If you need a rule of thumb, then in these modern times I would suggest you write more for those who relish dialogue than for readers who enjoy a well-turned phrase. Television is changing the way we think – and on the small screen, the spoken word is king (though still coming a long way behind the emperor known as 'action'!)

Balance is even less easy to quantify, or define. It has something to do with the aesthetic appearance of your story on the printed page, and a lot to do with pace – words fired like bullets excite tremendously. If there is nothing to say, then your characters must remain silent. Conversely, when you wish to impart information and keep your story progressing ever onwards, dialogue is often the best way – even if you must search for the apposite words.

The four functions are self-explanatory. I've already mentioned that there are restrictions inherent in any single character viewpoint, and it is partly by the skilful use of dialogue that these restrictions are overcome. By his involvement in conversation with other characters the viewpoint character becomes aware of incidents and events occurring elsewhere, or in the past. By giving each character a unique way of speaking the writer creates individuals, and by causing this speech to vary under conditions of stress the emotions experienced by all characters are successfully conveyed to the reader.

WHAT IS GOOD DIALOGUE?
If you were to write an overheard conversation directly into your story, it wouldn't make much sense. People talk in verbal shorthand. Your transcription would be riddled with false starts, meaningless sounds and sentences trailing away into thin air. To understand most normal conversations you need to be in a position to watch the speaker's face, note the gestures, and hear the various shifts of tone and emphasis

that help to convey meaning.

Your readers are not in that position. So good dialogue must be selective. Clarity is essential, ambiguity fatal. Good dialogue should be stamped with the speaker's character, so that the reader does not need constant reminding that George or Jean or Nigel is the person speaking.

Dialect should be used sparingly. No reader likes to struggle through conversations with spellings like a dictionary's phonetic pronunciation instructions. Throw in the occasional local expression, construct your sentences in a manner peculiar to the regional dialect you are portraying, spell the odd word here or there a little differently – and that should be sufficient.

He said and *she said* are used all the time, but if they appear tiresome then your thesaurus will provide many alternatives. But moderation is called for; nothing is worse than a page filled with *he growled, she snapped, he hissed* or *the thug gritted.* Very often the obtrusive *he said* is in the mind of the author, and completely unnoticed by the reader who is totally involved in an enthralling story.

In dialogue, the position of *he said* can be important. For example:

'What's that?' he asked.

With *he asked* in that position, we have an innocuous question. But with the construction altered …

'What,' he asked, 'is that?'

… we have something stronger, perhaps a little menacing, certainly charged with meaning.

Qualifying adverbs can be used with *he said*, but again, moderation is called for. Instead of saying, *she said hesitantly*, it is far better to construct your sentence so that the manner of delivery is unmistakable:

'Well,' she said, 'I don't know, I'm sure ... I suppose it's all right, but....'

Similarly, it's unnecessary to use, *he said sharply*, if, when the young lad comes in late from the disco his father's words are:

'You're late. Up to bed. Now!'

Adjectives can be used to describe the voice:

Her voice was *husky*, and *strangely disturbing* ...
As his anger rose his voice became *thin* and *brittle* ...
Her voice was *low* and *provocative* ...

The voice can be compared with sounds or objects recognizable to any reader, and which give a vivid impression of the voice's quality, or timbre:

He showed no mercy; each word cut like a *knife* ...
He spat each word out like a *sliver of ice* ...
She had a beautiful voice, as *musical as a mountain stream* ...

There is direct description:

His eyes flashed: he had difficulty keeping the temper out of his voice ...
When he replied he was almost choking with indignation ...
Her voice was pleasant, but the smile hadn't reached her eyes ...

and, finally, there are manner-of-delivery phrases:

'That's your problem,' he said *with grim intensity* ...
'Darling, your arm!' she gasped *with a quick look of*

concern ...
   'I made it myself,' he said *with smug satisfaction ...*

Motivation

Motivation can be looked at on several levels, and the most basic is exemplified by the early example of the poacher: he had discovered that he was the rightful heir to the estate, and this motivated him to steal the documents establishing his birthright.

You will find this level of motivation throughout your stories as your characters react to incidents and situations. But there is another, much deeper level, which has to do with a person's character. You will remember that I suggested it always helps to know a great deal about your main characters – much more, in fact, than you can ever write into your story. And I said that you need that knowledge to understand how your characters will react to certain situations.

If there is a confrontation in a pub, one man will punch his way out of it where another would use words. After a tiff with a girlfriend, one type of man would refuse to talk to her for weeks on end; another would turn up half an hour later with a bunch of red roses or a box of chocolates....

Once you know your characters, when a certain incident motivates them to act (our clown agreeing to step into the cage with an unpredictable lion) you will also understand the reason – the motivation – that makes them act the way they do. Your characters will be believable, because (if you have done your job) your readers will be one step ahead of you, and be anticipating your characters' actions.

Flashback and Transitions

Most of the techniques discussed so far can be used almost anywhere in our short story. For example, VIEWPOINT and DIALOGUE can be in use from the moment pen touches paper: your story can actually open with a line of dialogue spoken by the viewpoint character – no bad way to start.

The same cannot be said of FLASHBACK and TRANSITION. Characters must be introduced and some sort of story line established before flashback can make any sense; and because transition is the technique of moving a story from place to place, or forward in time, it follows that the same principle applies and a writer must be well into a story before its use becomes necessary.

You will have noticed that both techniques manipulate time. Because of this, unless they are handled skilfully, the reader can easily become confused.

Flashback is almost always necessary at some stage in the writing of a short story. Usually, you will begin your story at a dramatic point in the plot structure. Your protagonist (main character) will be in a mess. To explain how the situation came about you must go back in time and tell your readers about events that have already taken place; why that man is hanging over a cliff, why the hero is robbing a bank, why the young girl is handing in her notice. You must do all of that without interrupting the flow of your story, and without confusion. Your readers must know the instant you step out of the main story line and go back in time, and must be prepared and ready for the moment of your return.

Flashback helps give a short story the illusion of depth. Because of its length, a short story necessarily covers a brief period of time. By using flashback, an author can appear to overcome this limitation by giving the impression that a greater time span has been covered.

Always remember that flashback should be used to recall only those incidents in the past that have a direct bearing on the story.

Always ensure that the flashback sequence is smoothly blended into the flow of narrative and dialogue, and that it is used at the right time. For example, it would be pointless to slip into a flashback sequence in the middle of an exciting car chase, simply to tell the reader that the villain's uncle had cut him out of his will. The fact itself might be relevant – it could explain the villain's avarice – but the car chase would hardly be the right place to insert the flashback.

How to Handle Flashback

There are several devices used by the skilled writer to slip smoothly into a flashback sequence. The simplest of these is the 'tell me':

> Colin stared up at his father, his eyes wide. 'Tell me about it!' he cried. 'Go on, dad, tell me!'
>
> So his father told him how it had been during those last, bitter months, how the tanks had rolled and the men had died and the glamour of war had been washed away in the black trench mud....

A song can help a character recall the past:

> She stopped, suddenly, as if struck by a giant fist. The music drifted out through the open window and she was carried back six long months, to another similar garden in another, brighter town....

A forgotten name, suddenly mentioned, can send a character's thoughts drifting backwards:

> 'Jane,' he said, smiling as he took her hand. 'So you're Jane ...' His lips framed the words mechanically as his mind slipped away to the other Jane he had said goodbye to that bright, moonlit night....

One technical point over which the student writer often gets confused is the question of which tense to use in a flashback. Most stories are written using the past tense, and to be accurate a flashback would need to go something like this:

She *had* been at university and *had* met Bill one bright, sunny afternoon. He *had* been walking across the campus, and she *had* noticed at once his dark good looks, his bold manner. She *had* smiled shyly....

Obviously, there are too many *hads*, and the right way to handle it is to use one or two *hads* to let the reader know you are using flashback, but once the flashback becomes indistinguishable from the present (or establishes its own present) then dispense with them and proceed in the simple past tense:

She had been at university and had met Bill one bright, sunny afternoon. He was walking across the campus, and she noticed at once his dark good looks, his bold manner. She smiled shyly....

Transition Techniques

Transition takes place more frequently than flashback. It will probably happen several times in your story as your characters move from place to place and as time passes. Your story must always be advancing, and a transition is a movement – either of place, in time, or both.

Like flashback, transition should blend smoothly into your story. Again, confusion must be avoided. The reader must be warned that a transition is about to take place, must be aware when it does take place, and must to some extent be prepared for the next scene, if the location has changed.

The warning that a transition is about to take place can be very simple, perhaps along these lines:

As Millicent drove home, tired but happy, realization dawned: in twelve hours time she would be starting work alongside the man she loved. The thought made her tingle with anticipation....

Or:

> 'Goodnight Dave, see you tomorrow.'
> 'Uh huh. Not me!'
> 'You're kidding! You got the day off?'
> I shook my head, grinned, then glanced ostentatiously at my watch. 'Nope, not the day. The whole week. In eight hours I'll be on that plane to the Bahamas – and I can hardly wait....'

STANDARD WORDS AND PHRASES
The actual transition can be indicated by the use of stock words and phrases. Indeed, it is often difficult to effect a transition without them. Examples are: The next morning; That evening; Just one hour and three beers later; and so on. Don't be afraid to use these simple devices. They work well.

A GAP IN THE PAGE
The easiest of all. If your story is double-spaced (as it should be), then leaving a space twice that size – perhaps with three dots centralized – will tell your reader that time has passed.

EMOTION
Emotion can effectively bridge the gap in time by closing one scene, and opening the next:

> Unable to think, he sat there, his mind numb.
> He was still sitting there, staring blindly into space, when....

AN OBJECT
An object can be used in the same way:

> I sat down, my legs suddenly weak, the diary hanging limp in my hand....
> I was still holding the diary when....

NATURAL ELEMENTS

... the storm broke, and thunder rumbled directly overhead.
Thunder was still rumbling faintly in the distance when....
The last thing he remembered was the angry sea, and the
white, foaming crests of the waves....
All that had changed when he regained consciousness. Now,
the flat, ugly swell barely rocked the boat....

I think the important point about any transition is to keep
it simple. Remember to lead the reader into it, so that the
change isn't unexpected, and then use one or more of the
above devices, or others you have noticed or devised. The
simplest are the gap in the page and the stock phrase. If you
use nothing else, you cannot go far wrong.

Style

The various techniques we have looked at in this and the
previous chapter can, to a certain extent, be given basic rules
to serve as a rough guide for the novice writer. But style is
something that develops as you practise your writing, and
because every style is unique, there can be no rules.

You will always be comfortable when writing in the style
that comes naturally to you, but you will find the going
extremely difficult when you try to adopt another style
because you are not succeeding, or because you want
to tackle another market. (You will remember that I advised
against studying published stories in order to achieve a sale
by aping their style.)

In Chapters 7 and 8 many of the points we have discussed
so far will be demonstrated by reference to one of my own
published stories. The story is some 6,000 words long, yet
was written very quickly, with virtually no changes. I didn't
consciously work out how I was going to write it. When I sat
down with the rough plot by my side the words began to flow
because I was writing in the style that has evolved over the
pasty thirty-something years. Evolved. Not deliberately

chosen and painstakingly practised, but allowed to develop and mature in a perfectly natural process.

I haven't put a name to my style, but I do know that when I write thrillers I am a different person, and find the going tough. I think it works; certainly I have sold thriller short stories. But it is never easy.

Don't make the mistake of working at your style. The best, indeed the only advice I can give you, is always to write your socks off. Never write *down* because you think the publication for which your story is intended will not accept good writing. It will.

And when you do achieve the first sale (as you will, sooner or later) you want to be able to read your story with the pride that comes from knowing that it is your finest work – until your next....

6   You and Your Reader

Before moving on to Chapter 7 and the study of the way an actual short story was written, I think it's worth taking a closer look at you, the people who are going to read your stories, and the various factors that will – to a certain extent – influence the quality of the writing you produce.

As far as you are concerned, this business of writing must be taken seriously if you are to succeed. There is only one way of learning to write, and that's by writing, and you must look at how that can be done without disrupting a schedule that is almost certainly crowded, and has probably been followed for many years.

Although you are unlikely to meet many of your readers, the relationship between you will be a close one. I've already pointed out that with every story you write you are risking revealing something of your inner self to an audience of many thousands. But each of those people is an individual, and between the two of you there is a one-sided exchange that is nevertheless more intimate than a conversation. You are revealing your thoughts in a way you would rarely do in a face-to-face situation, and although you are unable to see or judge their reaction, if you have done your job well your readers will experience a wide range of emotions.

There is a beginning and an end to this process. It starts in your place of work, and finishes as the reader leans across and replaces the magazine on the coffee table. Through the story you have created, your readers learn – or believe they learn – something about you. And in order to do your job

properly, before you put pen to paper you should try to
know something about those readers you have never met.

In this chapter we will look at:

- Time
- Place
- Organization
- Word processors
- Reference books
- The reader
- A unique partnership

Time

As a novice writer you will probably have a full-time job that
takes up most of your day. If you are married and have a
family, then you know that what you think of as *your* spare
time is not necessarily your own. When you do make
breathing space, other tasks will clamour for attention. And
if, eventually, you find the time to sit down at your desk, the
chances are that you will feel too tired to write.

Robert Louis Stevenson is reputed to have written *The
Strange Case of Dr Jerkyll and Mr Hyde* over one terrible
weekend when he was racked with pain, haemorrhaging,
and reclining on his sick-bed in a darkened room. I mention
it because when I think of him accomplishing that task under
those circumstances, and with a dip pen and ink, it offers me
encouragement – or should I say that (for a while) it makes
me ashamed of the pitiful excuses I (sometimes) find for not
writing.

The love of writing will drive you on, I know that. But
even with high-minded principles and the burning desire to
succeed you must still work to make writing time, and how
you do that depends to some extent on your body clock, and
possibly your ability to write under any conditions. For
instance, are you an early bird, or a night owl? Do you
always need a nap in the middle of the day? Can you write in

the middle of what seems like a riot? Are you able to stay awake – and concentrate – on the 9.30 to Paddington?

I've painted a somewhat grim picture when, in truth, most people do manage to find a certain amount of time for writing. How much time you can find is not as important as its regularity; constant daily practice is invaluable. If you can easily set aside an hour or so every day, try to make it the hour when you are least tired and most alert – and stick to it. That way, your mind will become accustomed to working with words at a set time of the day or night, and will be at its best.

However, if it already seems that there are not enough hours in the day, you must examine your busy schedule – with reference to your body clock – and see if there are minutes you can filch here and there. The morning train to work is one opportunity, but many people find that getting up an hour earlier is the best solution. Night people disagree, and stay up burning the midnight oil (whereas my grandmother always maintained that, where sleep is concerned, the hours before midnight are the most important). Others work during their lunch hour. House-wives – and nowadays househusbands – jot down a sentence or two while waiting for the potatoes to boil.

You must discover which suits you, and again make it an unvarying part of your daily routine. How long you spend writing is usually determined by circumstances. I've mentioned an hour, but you might manage much longer than that, or much less. And the number of words you complete in the time allotted will vary. People write at different rates, but a first draft is often completed quickly, whereas a second will probably take much longer and the third – when little more needs altering – can be the quickest of all.

But there is one rule over which all writers are in agreement: a regular time set aside for writing – even fifteen minutes a day – will always be more productive than intense bursts of writing broken up by long periods of inactivity.

Place

I've already touched on this subject when I suggested writing on the 9.30 to Paddington. And of course that was only partly tongue in cheek, for many writers do at least a portion of their work while commuting.

But that is usually in addition to the serious writing they do at home, and I suppose a short, hilarious article could be written about the many and varied places writers can be found bent over their typewriters. Wasn't it Roald Dahl who did most of his work in a shed at the bottom of the garden? I think it was – and perhaps the fantastic situations he wrote about were inspired because (so legend has it) down there by his unusual office, fairies dwell.

Unless you are fortunate, you will probably find that at first you write in your living-room, perhaps at a desk or writing bureau. Later, paperwork and files and reference books will begin to creep across the floor, and it's then that you must think seriously about a room of your own; a study, where television is unknown and where you can pick up exactly where you left off because you know nothing has been disturbed. A stereo system can be helpful; many people write better with a background of appropriate music.

Once you have your study or office, it becomes a matter of narrowing down this concept of place in order to position your desk. When there is a choice between a view or a blank wall, the usual advice is to choose the blank wall every time; a view distracts, they say, and if it's too attractive you'll spend your time gazing out of the window.

Something between the two is a good compromise. From time to time you will need to rest your eyes (very important if you are using a word processor), and if there is a window to one side overlooking green fields or a lawned garden you should spend a few minutes each hour with the focus of your eyes changed as you gaze at those restful colours. Eye strain will be relieved, headaches prevented – and you will have time to gather your thoughts.

Have important reference books within each reach. This is made easier if you have a swivel chair, but in any case ensure that the seat you use is comfortable, with good back support. Make sure the light is exactly right: neither too bright nor too dim, and positioned so that it shines onto your work without causing glare.

Organization

In the beginning you will have one story. A couple of thousand words.

Very little organization is needed.

But project your thoughts forward just two years and imagine that you have have been writing one story a fortnight – a very respectable output indeed – and have forty-eight stories filed away. Some will have been published, others will be unsold, but all will have a history. And to keep a record of each story's history you will need an efficient filing system.

My original method of recording a story's comings and goings was to allot a page to each in a hard-backed notebook. The title of the story, its type (general, romance, thriller) and the number of words went at the top of the page, and pencil lines divided the rest of the sheet into columns for the date the story was submitted, the magazine it was sent to, the result, and any payment.

Later I progressed to a standard index card system, and I now use a database – which is just a fancy way of saying an index card system on a computer. But the layout of the page, or card, has remained exactly the same, because that's all the information you need: details of the story, where it's been, and if it sold.

When your stories do start selling, your financial affairs will need organizing. Your income from story sales is earned income, and as such taxable, but there will be certain expenses such as paper, typewriter ribbons, and some essential reference books that can be deducted to arrive at the true taxable income. There is no room in this book for a detailed look at the subject, but both *The Writers' and Artists' Yearbook* and *The Writer's Handbook* have sections dealing with income tax and the writer, while if your income increases dramatically it might be worth while employing an accountant.

Word Processors

I was introduced to word processors because an electronic typewriter I bought was unsuitable and my wife persuaded me to take the plunge. She knew me well. I was opposed to such modern, technological gadgetry, and ordered an Amstrad PCW8256 with some reluctance.

Now, five years on, I have the same wonderful computer with its memory doubled and an additional 3½'' disc drive, and as I go about my daily work I wonder how I ever managed without it.

Most people are familiar with the concept of a word processor, but some (usually non-writers) believe that the machine writes the story. What a word processor actually does is take the drudgery out of writing and leave the author free to get on with the creative work.

Any writer of my age will remember the days when a first draft was typed, amended by crossing out words and sentences and scribbling between lines and in margins, a second draft typed and the whole process repeated. This could go on through third and fourth drafts; and because everything was done manually, a writer would still be altering words and phrases as what was intended to be the final draft was being typed.

Now, a word processor allows the writer to amend on screen, and only when the story is exactly right is it sent to the publisher.

THE BASICS
If you decide that word processing is for you, you can buy a

perfectly adequate system for under £400. You need a monitor, keyboard and printer, and the word processing software (the programme that makes it all work).

For those new to computers it's best to look on them as machines that are not very clever, but that work very quickly and with great efficiency. While you are writing your story or editing an existing work, it resides in the computer's 'memory'; it is not permanent, and if you switch the computer off, your work is lost.

In this state your story is extremely malleable. You can alter words, delete bits you don't like, move blocks of text, insert sections from earlier drafts or from other stories, and incorporate embellishments such as italics, underlining, and bold print. Movement through a document is very fast. You can be working on the tenth page, skip instantly to page one to check on something you have written, and return to where you were.

From time to time as you write you will 'save' your work to disc. All this means is that by pressing certain keys your work is copied electronically onto a disc, and becomes permanent. Discs are 3½'' square and simply slot into the computer. I think of them as very roomy filing cabinets, because this is where all your work is stored. You can file your stories on different discs, and in different groups on each disc, so the way you organize your work is very flexible. And if you want a printed copy, you can print from the work currently in memory, or from any of the files (stories) on disc – at any time, and as many copies as you like.

There are many different makes of computer, but just three main types: IBM compatibles, Apple Macintosh, and Amstrad PCWs. The only time there is a problem is if you want to transfer your files from one to another – say, from an Amstrad PCW to an IBM compatible computer. This can be done, but requires extra software. Nowadays, editors often request work on disc, and it's a procedure that's likely to become very common. But at present, as far as most people are concerned they can work merrily away on whatever computer they have chosen, confident in the knowledge that each time they send a story out the printed copy will have no mistakes or alterations.

With the necessary attachments, work can be transmitted between computers via the normal telephone lines. The box of tricks required is called a modem, and it converts the information coming from your computer into a signal acceptable to the telephone system.

It has been said that because word processors make the production of impeccably printed copy so easy but cannot promote talent where none exists, a flood of second-rate stories and articles are swamping the market. Only editors themselves know how true that is. But for most writers, a word processor is the tool that enables them to get much closer to perfection – a proximity previously governed by the number of times they were prepared to retype.

Reference Books

It's usual to give lists of recommended reading in an appendix at the end of instructional books, and I have done just that. But I do feel that a brief look at some of the many reference books available will help you choose those that will be the most helpful, and the time you need those books at your elbow is now, as you begin to write your story.

DICTIONARIES
This is surely the reference book found on everyone's desk, but choosing one is not all that easy because I know for a fact that a dictionary one writer swears by, another wouldn't touch with a barge-pole.

I have three. The first is *The Concise Oxford Dictionary* (I've just replaced it – the first was falling apart). It is recommended by many experts, looks good on the shelf, and I'm entirely happy with it. My second – a recent acquisition – is the *Reader's Digest Reverse Dictionary*, which I still don't quite understand but use constantly to find names that are on the tip of my tongue: different parts of a castle, the various bits and pieces of a suit of armour, menu terms, French phrases, the components of a rifle, heraldry terms, and so on.

Another fine work of reference is *Chambers English Dictionary*. Many publishers consider it to be the most satisfactory – subject only to the availability of *The Oxford English Dictionary* – and it is another excellent choice.

DICTIONARIES OF QUOTATIONS

The Penguin International Thesaurus of Quotations, Everyman's Dictionary of Quotations and Proverbs – these and many others all have an index from which a key word is selected which leads to quotations in the body of the book that can enliven a piece of prose. One example: *In America only the successful writer is important, in France all writers are important, in England no writer is important, and in Australia you have to explain what a writer is.* (Geoffrey Cotterell, 1961)

THESAURUSES

I've just glanced in my *Concise Oxford*, and discovered that the alternative plural is thesauri!

Oh, well. Anyway, the *Reverse Dictionary* operates something like one of these, but when we mention this word (and not many of us do, because we can't pronounce it) we're usually talking about *Roget's*. This comes in many versions, but all provide synonyms and antonyms, often in contiguous sections: Cunning is followed by Artlessness: War follows Peace; Giving is followed by Receiving; and in each of the sections there are a number of nouns, adjectives and verbs, profusely cross-referenced, all broadly agreeing with the heading, but each with that fine shade of meaning that makes one exactly right in one context, and only nearly right in another.

The words are also grouped into classes: Abstract

Relations; Space; Matter; Intellect; and although these broad groupings make it a little easier to understand *Roget's* system, it's usually easier to find a particular word by looking in the detailed index.

The Oxford Thesaurus is another good one, in arrangement much more like a dictionary. There are many illustrative sentences in which words are shown in context.

ENGLISH USAGE

One stands out above all others: *Modern English Usage*, by H.W. Fowler, and if you are lost in the complexities of subjunctives, or wondering what to do with shall and will, or should and would, then this is where you should look. But there is another excellent alternative called *Usage and Abusage*, by Eric Partridge; and a little volume entitled *Write Right: A Desk Drawer Digest of Punctuation, Grammar and Style* by Jan Venolia, is a gem that deserves to be on every novice writer's shelf.

The Reader

Although I have stressed that there is little to be gained from writing stories that are carbon copies of magazine stories you have read, you must at least have some idea of the type of reader likely to appreciate your work.

If you are writing stories for the women's magazines, you must take account of age, and lifestyle: it takes but a moment's thought to realize that a story adored by a 16-year-old working girl is unlikely to appeal to a wealthy septuagenarian.

You can judge what section of the public a magazine is intended for by looking at the stories and articles it publishes, and the type of advertisements it accepts.

Those men's magazines that do exist are mostly aimed at the younger set.

And if you write literary short stories, crime, or science fiction, then your potential readership will be of all ages, both sexes, and from all walks of life.

A Unique Partnership

Earlier, I said that the relationship between you and the reader you have never met is very close, and if we take that one step further you will discover that this affinity has a direct bearing on the amount of detail you put into your story. I will return to this theory again when commenting on the story you will read in the next two chapters, but what it means is that your reader is so in tune with you that one or two carefully chosen words can create a vivid picture.

Take these five simple words: *Ella walked into the kitchen.* The kitchen is not described, and for the moment it doesn't matter what picture is in the writer's mind. Each reader will look at those words and create in their own minds an image of a kitchen. One might see a Welsh dresser, an Aga cooker, a clothes airer hoisted by a pulley, a bowl of fresh vegetables on a wooden draining-board. Another will picture a gleaming modern kitchen with a microwave oven, a dishwasher, a tumble-drier, dishes glistening inside white kitchen units with leaded windows.

So there is a partnership at work here. A writer need only mention a room and one or two articles or pieces of furniture to evoke a clear mental image in the mind of his reader. An aspidistra in an ornate bowl alongside a dark hall stand puts the reader in a bygone age, while a micro-stereo CD player standing on a shelf next to a copy of *The Satanic Verses* and *Spycatcher* creates a modern setting and says something about the story's characters.

This partnership is unique. No matter how skilled the writer is at choosing words, the image in each reader's mind will be different. And in the mind of an adult, the picture can be extraordinarily detailed. Just imagine the pictures your own mind would conjure up if you read that the hero had stepped through a doorway and found himself in a crowded eastern bazaar where a snake-charmer sat cross-legged before a tall basket; a room where a blowzy woman slammed an iron kettle onto a blackened hob; another where a man slapped four aces onto the green baize and squinted through a haze of cigarette smoke.

And although in certain circumstances you must describe scenes in great detail, most of the time when writing a short story this unique empathy between you and your reader is a partnership that never fails to work its magic.

You will see exactly what I mean in the next chapter.

7 A Complete Short Story – With Instructive Commentary

Already we have covered a lot of ground. We have taken an overall look at short story writing, discussed the never-ending search for ideas, learned how to create a plot, and looked in some detail at a number of technical devices that enable a writer to tell a story in a convoluted way without confusing the reader.

But any examples used to explain the various principles expounded have either been invented for the purpose, or isolated from the original story. They have been of use, but may have lost some impact through being seen out of context.

In this and the next chapter I have attempted to remedy that minor irritation by presenting a complete short story, and at various points in it looking back and discussing the methods that have been used. The story is called *Caribbean Cool*, it sold first time out to *Woman and Home*, and was based on the following PLOTSKEL:

SITUATION

A simple Jamaican craftsman, Johnny Lomax, who cannot read or write, is in love with a beautiful girl called Melody.

Incident One

He haggles mercilessly with a customer in his workshop – not realizing it is the girl's father, Kieron Pritchard – a well-known writer.

Incident Two

Unable to face the man, he telephones to express his love for the beautiful Melody and ask for her hand in marriage. It is refused.

REACTION

A young street urchin known as Jacko the Lizard tells Johnny about a professional letter-writer called Solomon Penn, and he decides to consult him. When he does, he asks for a letter to be written so that he can state his case in a manner that will impress Kieron Pritchard.

FRUSTRATION

The letter is written, and sent to Kieron Pritchard's house. But now there is a problem. When Johnny Lomax arrives at the house he is shocked to see Jacko the Lizard there. And as he finds himself being accepted into the family, he now fears that all will be lost if Kieron Pritchard discovers how the letter was written.

REACTION/RESOLUTION

But it is Kieron Pritchard who apologizes to Johnny Lomax. He had ordered Jacko the Lizard to take Johnny Lomax to the professional letter-writer in order to get an assessment of his character – and Solomon Penn had accused him of wasting his time by sending a good man for unnecessary scrutiny. Kieron Pritchard admits to being a stubborn fool, and Johnny Lomax gets his girl.

My first considerations when starting to write the story were the viewpoint to use, and whether to opt for first or third person.

The choice was between Johnny Lomax – as the man with the problem – or the street urchin, Jacko the Lizard, used as a minor character watching the action. But one glance at the resolution stage shows that with Jacko as viewpoint character the story wouldn't work. Kieron Pritchard admits to Johnny Lomax that Jacko the Lizard had taken him to Solomon Penn at his bidding – so there is an important element of surprise that would be lost if the story was seen through Jacko's eyes.

There was no special reason for choosing third person – in fact, there was no conscious decision. But if you glance at the first paragraph you will see that through the use of third person I was able to introduce Johnny Lomax by name very early. In the first person, that same paragraph would read: *The tiny figure slipped from bright evening sunshine into the deep shadows of my workshop like the lizard after which it took its name, a flash of glistening brown skin all that I could see as I lifted tired eyes from the glittering metal bowl I held in my hands.* And, quite honestly, I don't think it works.

Two further points. Firstly, although the story runs to just over 6,000 words, you will notice that there are only five characters, and two of those appear but briefly. And secondly, although the problem is a familiar one, the fresh treatment of an old idea has created an original short story in a delightful setting.

Caribbean Cool

The tiny figure slipped from bright evening sunshine into the deep shadows of Johnny Lomax's workshop like the lizard after which it took its name, a flash of glistening brown skin all that Johnny could see as he lifted tired eyes from the glittering metal bowl he held in his hands.

'Hey, now,' he murmured softly. 'Was that a little biddy mote, a speck of brass twinkling in the sunlight? Or do I detect movement over there in the corner? Maybe ...' and here Johnny's eyes crinkled and he put down the ancient engraving tool to look about him with mock concern, '... maybe my workshop's all at once invaded by vermin, and I've gotta call on the old catcher man who'll come runnin' with his traps and his poisons....'

He was rewarded by a half-suppressed giggle; the rustle of paper; a sudden glimpse of a naked, dusty foot, the ragged edges of faded denim shorts.

Johnny heaved an exaggerated sigh of feigned disappointment. 'No, guess again, Lomax. It's just that young rascal, Jacko the Lizard, come to annoy an old man when he's too tired to defend himself; too low in spirits to care.'

'You're not old, Johnny, man.' The voice was flute-like, but strong, and the words – dripping with scorn – were accompanied by a roll of huge brown eyes, the whites visible even in the shadows. 'And just for you I've come runnin' all the way from the beach with hot news of Solomon Penn the Scribe – man, he's got mean skills that can lift your spirits from the depths of misery, move them to wherever you want them moved.'

'To the house of Kieron Pritchard, the Writer of Books?' Johnny asked, half smiling as he returned to his work.

'Absodefilutely, Johnny,' the voice piped gleefully. 'Where – as you well know – the beautiful Melody's starin' with moist eyes at the walls of her room, just waitin' for Johnny the Stupid to make his move –'

'Out!' Johnny cried in mock anger. The brass bowl clattered to the bench as he rose from his stool and made a lazy grab for the boy, to be rewarded by a peal of laughter and a blur of movement that left his fingers grasping nothing but the warm air. Johnny shook his head helplessly as Jacko squatted on his heels in the doorway with an impish smile playing about his lips.

I'm six foot tall, forty years old, I've got one knee like a seized-up hinge and I'm getting nowhere, fast, Johnny thought. My body aches with longing for a girl I can't have, and a skinny kid who darts like a lizard through the back alleys of Kingston is running me ragged.

Worse still, I was an arrogant, stubborn fool in front of the girl's father, and that leaves me clutching at the fragile straws this kid tosses my way. But ... maybe, just maybe, there could be something to be learned from this Solomon Penn feller, this scribe man who practises his skills on the hot white sands....

'I told old Kieron I was crazy with love for that girl,' Johnny said pensively. 'He turned me down flat. I'm a humble craftsman. The education I had ain't worth a handful of dust. But that Kieron, he's a writer of fine books and he's got an ohhhhh, soooo beautiful daughter....'

'You spoke like a fool,' Jacko agreed, and snapped his fingers derisively. 'That old phone's fallin' to bits, and you babbled like a man with a head as empty as a souvenir conch. Hey, Johnny, even from where I sat listening I could hear old Kieron laughing as you apologized, then begged for the hand of his daughter.'

'Only partly right, Jacko,' Johnny said gloomily. 'There was no beggin' involved, and he was polite, but totally dismissive – and I tell you, I can see the man's point. He wants more for his daughter than a man whose black hair's already turning grey – and who haggles for a full hour with him over a brass bowl worth nothing but the few ounces of metal it contains.'

'Ayah,' Jacko groaned, covering his eyes with his hands. 'That was crazy, Johnny. A man who wants to marry the daughter of a big-time writer sure don't rip him off, strip his wallet clean for a useless brass pot.'

'Hey, it's okay me knockin' my work, Jacko, but you lay off, you hear!' Johnny ordered. 'Fact is, that was a genuine Jamaican artefact, wrought with a whole lot of fine traditional skills. And at the time I'd no idea this fat guy with the padlock on his wallet was the father of the delicious Melody.'

'Please, Johnny, don't,' Jacko scoffed. 'You're breaking my heart.' and as a dilapidated old Ford Zephyr convertible rattled down the street trailing squeals of teenage excitement and clouds of white dust, he sneezed, and scampered from the doorway to sip cool water from the cloth-draped jug on Johnny's littered bench.

'This Solomon Penn, the Scribe,' Johnny urged softly. From a shelf he took down a bowl of sticky sweets, casually placed it within reach of the boy.

'And old, old man,' said Jacko the Lizard. His lips were moist. His eyes were everywhere but on the bowl of temptation.

'But nevertheless a man with priceless skills – you're saying – who at one fell swoop will cause the sun to shine for twenty-four hours of every day on my poor old love-life?'

Jacko shrugged. 'In a nutshell, Engraver, and taking full account of every damn swing and roundabout – abso-defilutely.'

And he shot out a thin brown arm, grabbed a handful of sweets, and scampered out into the fading sunlight.

The first thing to note about the beginning of *Caribbean Cool* is where it begins, in relation to the PLOTSKEL.

You will recall that in Chapter 4 we decided that our sailor story had started at Incident Two in its PLOTSKEL, while the Irish story used as a short example started at the REACTION stage. *Caribbean Cool*'s REACTION stage is when Johnny Lomax is told about the professional letter-writer by Jacko the Lizard – and that's where the story starts.

In fact that first scene covers but a small part of the REACTION stage, and it closes with Johnny Lomax doing no more than expressing guarded interest in the letter-writer.

At that point in the story there is a gap with three little dots, followed by a fresh scene – we have to a certain extent left the readers in suspense. Before we continue it's worth looking back to see how much has been achieved in a little over 900 words. And so that we have something to guide us, let's remind ourselves of what we must always set out to complete in the first few pages of any story:

1   Introduce the main character
2   Hint at the problem
3   Set the scene
4   Establish the mood
5   Cast the narrative hook

Johnny Lomax is in the story from the beginning, but it's interesting to note how he is described because it does two jobs simultaneously: describes Johnny, and hints at his problem.

I'm six foot tall, forty years old, I've got one knee like a seized-up hinge and I'm getting nowhere, fast, Johnny thought. My body aches with longing for a girl I can't have, and a skinny kid who darts like a lizard through the back alleys of Kingston is running me ragged.

The problem is mentioned several times: *I told old Kieron I was crazy with love for that girl ... he turned me down flat ... wants more for his daughter than a man whose hair's already turning grey ... who haggles for a full hour with him over a brass bowl....*

Although the location is finally pinned down in that self-descriptive paragraph, it is being set right from the beginning: *slipped from bright evening sunshine into the deep shadows of Johnny Lomax's workshop ... runnin' all the way from the beach ... The brass bowl clattered to the bench as he rose from his stool....*

And the mood is established by the gentleness of Lomax himself, as he murmurs softly, in the way his eyes crinkle as he looks about with mock concern. There is mock anger, a half-suppressed giggle. And as Lomax places the bowl of sweets within Jacko's reach we become involved in a story that is gentle, humorous, full of sunshine and laughter.

Is there a hook? I must admit that nowadays when I write a story the techniques I am discussing in this book come automatically. Reading through it now, I would suggest that Jacko the Lizard arriving *with hot news of Solomon Penn the Scribe* and his *mean skills* is intriguing, and is followed up a little later when Johnny muses that *there could be something to be learned from this Solomon Penn feller....*

In the next scene, we meet Johnny's girl....

*   *   *

In the dim light filtering through the curtained doorway Johnny kissed Melody tenderly, feeling as always the most exquisite trembling in his bones as he led her into the room to seat her gracefully on the rattan settee.

And there was pride, too. For Johnny was aware that about his tiny flat above the dusty workshop there was always an atmosphere of old colonial charm, which he'd carefully cultivated through judicious purchases on his visits to Kingston's many furniture and bric-à-brac markets.

'Sheer paradise,' Melody whispered now. She sighed and allowed the folds of her mauve chiffon scarf to slip silkily away from her dark hair and drape her naked shoulders, doing it with that charming dip of her head that Johnny knew was not shyness, but an unconscious mannerism that to him was captivating. 'Always, Johnny Lomax, I feel so much at home here. If my stubborn old Daddy could see this room....'

'If your dear old Daddy knew you were meeting me every evening, I'd be on the next boat out of Kingston, Melody,' Johnny said with absolute conviction.

He'd been courting the slim girl with the dancing eyes, always with great propriety, since late one glorious, wet afternoon when she'd slipped under his tattered golf umbrella as he was splashing awkwardly through dun-coloured main road puddles. She'd clutched his arm with slender fingers, and as her dark hair brushed his shoulder her throaty chuckle had sent shivers down his spine.

Embarrassment had been uppermost in his mind, but she'd soon put paid to that.

'This is the big, modern world,' she'd pointed out as she dragged him through the rush-hour traffic. 'If I'm caught in a downpour and you've got a brolly, man, we share – and the matter of our sex is neither here nor there.'

Well, that was where logic went whistling out of the window, as far as Johnny was concerned. For while he could understand that sharing his bright canopy of ragged cloth and broken ribs with a pretty girl was definitely the neighbourly thing to do, once Melody was pressing her warm breast to his arm as she held her thin cotton dress high and ran with him for the nearest shelter, then sex was there with a vengeance.

Early on he had learnt that her father would stand for no

hanky-panky of any kind between them. Somehow that had only added spice to the adventure. And as day followed day and the scorching heat of summer cleared the wide Jamaican skies, Johnny discovered that his own brand of street wisdom was winning hands down. Perceptibly, the look in Melody's liquid brown eyes had turned from brash friendship to the beginnings of a shy, intense love – and from the day she had blushingly confessed her feelings to him, they had shared late afternoon iced tea in the cramped flat above the workshop, and basked in the glow of 'making plans'.

Which always came shuddering to a halt against the unseen but absolutely immovable bulk of her daddy, Kieron the Writer.

From the beginning, Melody had kept her daddy fully informed about the man she was seeing; had later confessed that she loved Johnny, and asked permission to bring him to her home.

But her candour had tragically rebounded. Soon after meeting Johnny, she told her daddy that this man she loved so deeply was a craftsman who exercised his rare skills in a tiny workshop, could neither read nor write, but would make her a fine husband.

And Kieron, to his discredit, had listened with interest to the first two details, and totally ignored the third.

Now, from a bamboo tray on the elegant pine dresser, Johnny took a delicate china pot and strained cold tea onto ice-cubes crushed into tall glasses, handed one to Melody and sat opposite her.

'This evening,' he said, 'would surely be the most wonderful evening of my life if you could tell me he's had a change of heart, Melody.'

'Not possible, Johnny,' Melody said, and he marvelled at her positive words, her ultra-modern way of getting straight to the blunt point of things. She was twenty-nine, highly intelligent, and *gorgeous*. He guessed her looks came from her late mother, her brains from Kieron and the formative years she'd spent at university. And because of that background, he could never understand why her heart had been stolen by a humble man who made his daily bread by scratching lines on brass bowls.

As he watched her, she sipped the cold tea, then shook her head sorrowfully. 'You know the way he is, Johnny. He's a talented man, and he considers lesser mortals to be....'

She hesitated, frowning, and quietly Johnny said, 'As beneath his contempt? Or perhaps as dangerous people possessed of a low cunning which he doesn't quite understand, and therefore fears?'

Melody sighed. 'You see, Johnny. That's what I'm always telling him. You left school early, yet every word you utter suggests you have a profound knowledge of life....'

'And – who knows – my low cunning may yet be his undoing.'

Startled, Melody slopped cold tea, the ice rattling in her glass as she brushed away his attempts to mop up the spillage.

'There, now you've worried me.' Her smile was sweetly flustered as she put down the glass, dipping her head and patting suddenly flushed cheeks with the tips of her fingers. 'Not that I'm accusing you of being cunning, Johnny. That word has the wrong connotations when applied to so gentle a man. But like a sleeping volcano you have hidden depths, my sweet. If you're led to believe that certain actions will lead to desired results....'

'*Led* to believe, Melody?' he queried, a smile twitching his lips at the thought that Johnny, the small-time engraver, should present the image of a smouldering volcano.

'If there is any cunning to be found, Johnny,' Melody said, dark eyes lingering on his face, 'then I am certain it must come from others.'

Johnny sighed, smiled a beatific smile, and mentally crossed his fingers. 'Then, with absolute honesty I can put your mind at rest. The only person to cross the threshold today was a kid without malice in his soul – and if there was an ounce of cunning there, all he used it for was to extract from me the stickiest sweets in Kingston.'

As he sliced thick, glistening wedges of melon, Johnny knew that though they had grown to be pretty close during the hot weeks of summer, still there were some things he must keep from her.

He sensed that it would be wrong to confess that in the

early evening he had downed tools and limped as fast as his leg would allow him through the maze of alleys behind his workshop in pursuit of Jacko the Lizard.

And to tell her that at dawn the next day he would be led – yes, that damn word – to the shimmering white sands washed by the blue waters of the Caribbean to discuss with an eccentric scribe called Solomon Penn certain underhand methods of bringing Kieron the Writer to heel was out of the question.

As Jacko would say, absodefilutely.

Maybe, when the deed was done....

We've already seen one transition – we moved from Johnny Lomax's workshop to his flat by the simple expedient of leaving a gap in the page filled with nothing but three small dots. There was no warning, other than a satisfactory end to the scene as Jacko scampered off into the fading sunlight.

There is a transition at the end of this scene, too, but this time there is some preparation. It comes in the last five-line paragraph, where Johnny ruminates on the next day's planned meeting with Solomon Penn.

This scene also provides the first instance of flashback. You will remember that I warned against flashback being used until the story was well underway, and in *Caribbean Cool* the opportune moment arrives when Johnny Lomax recalls his meeting with the delightful Melody.

The movement into the flashback sequence comes with: *He'd been courting the slim girl ... since late one glorious, wet afternoon ...*; and we move out of it with: *now, from the bamboo tray....*

The dialogue in both these scenes has been a valiant attempt to portray not necessarily an authentic Jamaican patois, but certainly conversation with a lilting cadence spattered with slang and dropped consonants. The standard *said* has been interspersed with *murmured, cried, piped, agreed, groaned* and *scoffed*, and among the qualifying adverbs used are *softly, gleefully, pensively* and *gloomily*.

Finally, before moving on, just a quick word about that unique partnership that was mentioned in Chapter 6.

At the beginning of *Caribbean Cool* the reader is taken into *the deep shadows of Johnny Lomax's workshop*, while in the second scene Johnny's flat over the workshop is only briefly described: *dim light filtering through the curtained doorway ... the rattan settee ... old colonial charm ... furniture and bric-à-brac*.

Yet because the writer has chosen his (few) words well, readers fill in with their imagination those details – purposely, cleverly? – left out, and create in their mind a picture that is acceptable, and satisfying. The workshop they see is partly the writer's creation, but mostly their own imagination; and mention of a rattan settee will evoke images that spread far beyond that simple piece of furniture and create an atmosphere that is derived from images stored in the mind over a great many years.

A television production rarely works so well. The leading character on screen – carefully chosen by the casting department – will appeal to some viewers, but not to all; and although the sets may be authentic, viewers will look at them with a critical eye, and not all will approve.

Right, on to the next scene.

The transition from Johnny Lomax's flat – involving movement in place and time – is again effected by a gap in the page. But this time the reader has been prepared, firstly by the conversation between Johnny and Jacko in the first scene (in the workshop), and secondly by Johnny's introspection at the end of the scene with Melody. This is the way the story continued:

> The Underwood typewriter was massive and black, its name emblazoned in crazed gold lettering. Its keys were as readable as worn fingerprints, as stained and misaligned as the teeth of an ageing alligator.
>
> It stood on a rickety wooden table. Alongside it were a grubby pile of bond typing paper, a battered Players Medium tobacco tin containing used paperclips and crumbling

fragments of gum eraser, a Golden Shred marmalade jar bristling with pens and pencils. Balanced on several of those pencils, like rakishly tilted leprechaun's hats, were mouldering green finger covers from which long use had worn most of the rubber pimples.

The table's splayed legs were firmly planted in the fine white sand. Here and there, stiff blades of coarse grass poked through, stabbing the heavy silence. Shells were scattered about: the cracked trumpets of twisted conch; the colourful globes of spiky sea urchins whose delicate pastel shades were picked out by the rays of the early morning sun as it struggled to break through the hanging sea mists.

High above, bedraggled palm fronds were limp green rags in the hot, still air.

The silence was broken by a faint plop as Jacko the Lizard tossed a pebble into the translucent waters that lazily lapped the sands.

Johnny stirred. Squatting with his back against the slender trunk of a palm, he was concerned about the ache in his bad knee. And he was becoming increasingly uncomfortable under the unwavering gaze of Solomon Penn, the Scribe.

'It's not so much a deception, man,' he said amiably, answering a question that was now so old as to be almost forgotten. 'I'd suggest – with respect, Sol – that it's more the honest effort of an uneducated man to create a favourable impression.'

Much earlier, Johnny had been led by the boy through a maze of alleys, eventually stumbling out onto the broad expanse of sand with his bare feet sorely bruised from contact with splintered boards, discarded tin cans, the scattered detritus of past decades.

Clear salt air washed away the stench of decay. Early morning joggers were patches of dazzling colour moving languidly against a backdrop of hazy light and shade. And as Johnny and Jacko the Lizard trudged across this dreamlike landscape, Solomon Penn, the Scribe, had appeared before them silhouetted against the washed-out horizon like a dark sculpture in delicate paper; an assembly of curves and angles and flat planes of such mystic beauty that it left Johnny awestruck.

But his was a simple tale, and despite a daunting feeling of inferiority he had told it well.

He wanted a letter, Johnny said. He couldn't read or write, so someone must write it for him. It must be written as if he, Johnny, had written it. It must explain his love for Melody, his willingness and ability to support her. And, if he approved of what was written, Johnny would sign it, and send it by express post.

Once or twice his courage had needed bolstering by sharp pokes from Jacko's bony elbows. But he had been proud of his performance, and when his voice finally dried up, suddenly so lost in the stillness that for the life of him he could not remember one single word, he had been stunned to hear Solomon Penn suggest that what he proposed was nothing more nor less than a cunning confidence trick.

Now, listening to Johnny's explanation, Solomon Penn pursed his lips.

Incongruously, he was seated behind the flimsy table in a heavy swivel chair whose taut, scuffed leather was edged with tarnished brass studs. Each time he moved – which, Johnny had noticed, was an exceedingly rare occurrence – the chair's dry bearings squealed like the brakes of his own rusting Raleigh.

The scribe was completely bald, yet blessed with a magnificent beard. Bright black eyes glistened above struggling silver curls that cascaded from high cheekbones the colour of fine charcoal to envelop utterly his chin and neck. His ragged jeans were cut off above the ankle, exposing broad feet resting on the turned chair legs from which the casters had long since rotted away. His torn yellow T-shirt had no sleeves. Thin gold bracelets glittered on arms that were like dark, shiny bones.

'The complicated splitting of hairs can't alter the truth, Johnny,' Solomon Penn stated. His voice ebbed and flowed, rattling like distant palm fronds in an on-shore breeze.

'But written words selected with care can paint pretty potent pictures in the mind of an educated man,' Johnny suggested.

'Deliberately contrived illusions to further one's own ends?' suggested Solomon Penn, his eyes twinkling.

'No, man. Just gentle persuasion. With – it must be admitted – that same admirable objective,' said Johnny. And as he sensed a softening of the scribe's manner, he was suddenly swamped by powerful waves of exultation.

Jacko the Lizard also sensed the change.

With a deft flick he sent a flat pebble skimming across the surface of the water. He padded lightly towards the table. Teeth flashed white as he stuck out his tongue, licked his grimy thumb and slid the top sheet of bond paper from the pile. Leaning across the unmoving Solomon Penn, he wound the sheet of paper into the typewriter. In the hot, still air, the rotation of the paper feed knob was like the chatter of far-off gunfire.

Johnny felt a surge of excitement as Solomon Penn reached up to pull thoughtfully at his beard with one gnarled hand. Fascinated, he watched the other drift forward to hover like a hawk over the old Underwood's keys.

The first sharp tap as a letter was printed on the paper made him jump. Jacko the Lizard giggled. He was leaning forward, elbows on the canted table, chin resting in his hands. His dark eyes flicked rapidly between the paper and the grizzled face of Solomon Penn.

The printing of the second letter was expected, but still startling in the silence. A third was rapped out, again with the finger of that one hand, while Solomon Penn gazed with unseeing eyes at the drifting sea mists and composed, in his head, the missive that would present to Kieron Pritchard the impeccable credentials of Johnny the Engraver, ardent suitor of his nubile daughter, Melody.

He's on his way, Johnny thought triumphantly. Sol the Scribe's telling my tale the way it should be told, playing that scintillating keyboard the way keyboards were played long before they became scintillating. And as the other hand slid away from the beard to join the fray and the tempo of Solomon's typing increased, Johnny clasped his hands around his knees to still their trembling, listened idly to the music of the keys and allowed his mind to drift into a blissful daydream in which all his problems had been solved.

And yet....

'The one insurmountable problem,' Solomon Penn was

saying in his dry husk of a voice, 'is that as you can't read, Johnny, you've got no way of knowing what I have written.'

Johnny blinked. Time had passed. The typewriter had stopped its clatter. And as he sluggishly dragged his mind from a pink, euphoric haze to a sandy present that was still fraught with uncertainty, he felt a faint but unmistakable sinking of the spirit.

Valiantly, he rallied.

'Which, in essence, Sol, makes an absolute pig's ear of your accusations of deceit,' he pointed out. 'We both already know I can't read, so the whole damn letter is your uncheckable composition – and I've got to put my mark to it in complete and utter trust.'

For a moment there was a look in Solomon Penn's dark eyes which Johnny could only interpret as dawning respect – though for the life of him he couldn't understand why. Then, with a grave nod of acquiescence, Penn winked broadly at Jacko the Lizard who, with studied flamboyance, ripped the paper from the typewriter and slapped it ceremoniously on the table.

From the marmalade jar with its peeling label, Solomon Penn selected a sleek bamboo holder with a blackened nib. From the jumble on the rickety table he produced a caked container of Indian ink. The stopper squeaked, mouselike, as he withdrew it. Dark blobs spattered the white sand.

To Johnny, the typewritten sheet was a maze of black squiggles that shimmered like a thousand tiny spiders in the heat. Also, with some misgivings he noted that the letter was much shorter than he'd expected.

Nevertheless, he was astute enough to realize that the composition had a beauty that the writer in Kieron Pritchard would appreciate. And if the message it conveyed was fifty per cent accurate, then that surely was a hundred per cent better than his own lovelorn status quo.

So with a deep feeling of humility, and of destiny in the making, Johnny took the proffered pen, dipped the nib in the thick black ink, and with an extravagant flourish scrached his simple mark on the paper.

And then, unable to contain his delight, he flipped the pen high into the air, let out a whoop of pure joy, and danced a gay jig around the table, his naked feet kicking up such clouds of fine sand that Solomon Penn hastily ripped off his T-shirt and spread it over the ancient Underwood.

On Jacko the Lizard, the flapping yellow cloth had the effect of a starter's flag. As if he had been trembling in anticipation of just such a signal he tore off his clothes, raced brown and naked across the sand into the glassy sea, and in a whirling flurry of arms and legs thrashed the flat surface into a wild, white foam.

You have probably read that in a short story there is no room for lengthy descriptive passages. If a story is 2,000–3,000 words long, that's probably true. But with experience you will learn that hard and fast rules have no place in writing, and a delightful piece of descriptive prose that does nothing but hold up the action in the shorter tale (and is therefore to be discarded) will fit perfectly into the longer story – and contribute greatly to the effect.

Establishing the mood and setting the scene must be achieved early in your story. But both will change, and while your story is unlikely to alter so drastically that a gentle romantic tale becomes a cold-blooded thriller, the scene of the action will move – as here – from a cluttered workshop to a cool, shady apartment, and then to a sun-soaked beach.

And in this scene the quite lengthy passage at the beginning re-establishes the mood, places the reader smack in the middle of an exotic, tropical setting and – very important – with that big black Underwood typewriter it edges towards the introduction of Solomon Penn, the Scribe, and begins to give the reader an inkling of his character.

There is another long flashback scene, and I want to draw your attention to this one because it illustrates my instruction on the use of tenses. You will recall that the way to move into a flashback is to use the compound past tense – had seen, had walked, had decided – for two or three lines, and then switch to the simple past tense – saw, spoke, walked, decided. And that's exactly how this one is handled.

There is a hint that a flashback is coming when Johnny answers a question *so old as to be almost forgotten*, and it begins with: *Much earlier Johnny had been led....* After that, 'had' is virtually done away with.

But not quite, and for good reason.

If a flashback scene is long – in short story terms – then it is advisable to throw in the occasional 'had' to remind the reader that, temporarily, you have stepped back in time. So in this paragraph:

> Clear salt air washed away the stench of decay. Early morning joggers were patches of dazzling colour moving languidly against a backdrop of hazy light and shade. And as Johnny and Jacko the Lizard trudged across this dreamlike landscape, Solomon Penn, the Scribe, *had appeared* before them silhouetted against the washed-out horizon like a dark sculpture in delicate paper; an assembly of curves and angles and flat planes of such mystic beauty that it left Johnny awestruck.

... you have the simple past tense – *washed, trudged* – and then as a brief reminder that this is a flashback sequence the solitary *had appeared* is thrown in.

I'm well aware that throughout this book I've made little mention of the beginning, middle and end of a story. Some theories suggest that you should always think of your story in terms of those three sections, writing a set number of words for each one based on a percentage of the whole – perhaps a 25%–50%–25% split. My own feeling is that as you tell the story constructed around your original PLOTSKEL you will naturally have a beginning section in which information necessary for your readers' understanding of the story is given, and where the readers are – as it were – invited to sit back and enjoy the show; a middle section in which much of the action occurs; and a shorter final stage in which the climax is reached and the story is resolved.

Using those criteria, *Caribbean Cool*'s beginning ends when the readers have been introduced to Melody, and

Johnny has forewarned them that the next day he will visit Solomon Penn. The middle starts immediately with that big, black, Underwood typewriter, and is still in full flow. I'm not sure when we reach what could be called the ending. I am re-reading the story with you as I write, so I think the best thing we can do is to move on to Chapter 8 and decide – between us – where that imaginary line lies....

8   The Short Story – A Continuation

This final, big scene begins with a flashback.

When discussing this technique in Chapter 5 I said that flashback would be necessary in most short stories because the readers need information about events that have already happened. The readers need that information because we begin our stories at a convenient high point in order to grab their interest. And although this next scene is not the beginning of the story, flashback is used for that same reason.

The familiar gap in the page was the transition (again across time and space), but if we had joined Johnny as he was mounting his bicycle for the ride across Kingston, followed him through the cool passages of Kieron Pritchard's house and out onto the marble terrace, we would have been asking our readers to stay with us on a journey – in the middle of our story – during which *nothing at all happened*.

Instead, we start the scene with a 'hook' that will hold the reader – *Johnny's heart was betraying him*. I call it a hook because at the time I wrote that part of the story I hoped that it would intrigue readers, they would want to know why, and there are repeated references to that problem as our flashback sequence takes us quickly across town to our first meeting with Kieron Pritchard. Only then do we learn what is causing Johnny such consternation: the presence of Jacko the Lizard, serving drinks with a sly smirk....

Caribbean Cool – Continuation

Johnny's heart was betraying him.

It had sustained him on the uncomfortable, five mile bicycle ride through the dusty Kingston streets to the peaceful suburbs where the rich had their palatial mansions.

And he had detected nothing more than the customary delicious fluttering – followed by the disconcerting feeling of his legs turning to water – when Melody, flushed and bubbling with happiness, had met him at the front door, taken his perspiring face in her hands, and kissed him full on the mouth with total disregard for the sensitivities of her daddy's important neighbours.

He had even managed to recover some semblance of dignity while following her silently through cool tiled passages with pale walls hung with rich oil paintings; through graceful flat arches leading to spacious rooms furnished with leather chesterfields where genuine tiger-skin rugs lay glassy-eyed beneath lazily rotating ceiling fans.

And when she led him onto a marble terrace of breathtaking beauty, across whose ornamental stone balustrades were visible lush gardens ablaze with bougain-villaea, graceful palms and, beyond, the limpid waters of the Caribbean which the light of the setting sun had turned a soft, flamingo pink, he had managed to meet Kieron Pritchard – cool hands, a hint of expensive aftershave, dark eyes that were not hostile – without betraying for a single moment the turmoil that was threatening to bring him to his knees.

But now, there was trouble.

For when they had settled into rattan chairs arranged around a glass-topped bamboo table and Kieron had snapped his fingers to summon refreshing drinks, who should come through from the depths of the house madly pushing a trolley jingling with bottles and glasses – but a slyly smirking Jacko the Lizard.

'A ... just a tonic water,' Johnny blurted, conscious that his mouth had been hanging open and both Melody and her daddy were watching him. Melody with an understandably quizzical look on her face, he noted – but Kieron with a most surprising look of genuine amusement.

Why? thought Johnny, accepting the heavy-cut glass from the grubby hands of Jacko the Lizard. Is there something in that letter written by Solomon Penn that has made me a figure of ridicule?

But if so, why am I now welcome in this house? And, most perplexing of all, how can Jacko the Lizard be making himself completely at home here? A Kingston street urchin, making like he owns the place?

Across from him, Kieron Pritchard drained his glass and sighed with deep contentment. Then he leaned forward, and from the table he took into his exquisitely manicured fingers – with unmistakable reverence – a brass bowl which Johnny had not noticed, but which he now instantly recognized as the one whose price he had stubbornly refused to discount.

So, why reverence? Johnny thought; and his confused mind reeled. 'You've ... er ... examined it, Kieron?' he asked weakly.

A smile played about Kieron's lips. 'Daily,' he said in wonderfully rich tones. 'And with increasing interest. I'm beginning to believe it really is worth the astounding sum you tried to extract from me....'

Johnny felt numb. Not only was he confronted with the glittering object that figured frequently in recent nightmares, but it seemed he'd been wrong about Kieron the Writer.

In his lightweight linen suit he cut an elegant figure without an ounce of fat in sight. There might even, Johnny dared to hope, be a spark of humanity within him which had been fanned into glorious life by the letter written on the Kingston sands....

'But I'm also intrigued,' Kieron was saying. 'I've been following the designs engraved around the bowl, and it seems to me....'

He fumbled in his jacket pocket, extracted a spectacle case, and perched the gold half-frames on his nose.

'Yeah, go on,' Johnny prompted. 'It seems to you....'

'It seems to me that there is history here, Johnny,' Kieron said, his finger tracing the network of fine engravings. 'Yet I was under the impression....' He stopped, and peered at Johnny, a puzzled frown creasing his brow.

'Steady, Daddy, you're allowing your prejudices to show,' Melody warned softly.

'Nonsense.' Kieron spread his hands, proclaiming his innocence. 'If I'm an educated, talented writer and this man's not, that's not prejudice, Melody – it's fact.'

He turned to Johnny and again leaned forward, elbows on the knees of his sharply-creased trousers, the brass bowl cupped in one palm. 'What I am saying to you, Johnny – and with much respect – is that I'm not only totally impressed with the skill of your workmanship, but I'm astounded by your obvious profound knowledge of Jamaican history.'

Johnny felt dazed. He sipped his drink, listened to the distant rattle of the drinks trolley as Jacko the Lizard wheeled it away, was vaguely aware of Kieron Pritchard talking softly to Melody, and then, somehow, he lost the thread ...

... and the next thing he knew with absolute certainty was that he was standing with Kieron by the ornamental balustrade – and the man's arm was around his shoulders.

'Come, Johnny,' the deep voice was saying. 'I have the general drift, but I need you to take me on a magical guided tour through these wonderful scenes you have created.'

Johnny looked about him. They were alone. From somewhere there drifted a faint sizzling, the tantalizing aroma of fine cooking. Pools of soft light from the many lanterns fell on the rich marble of the terrace. The shallow brass bowl glistened like pale gold in the light of the rising moon.

He shook himself mentally, and feeling as if somehow he had walked into a dream, he took the bowl from Kieron the Writer and with trepidation began to describe the scenes he had, with much patience, engraved in the soft metal.

'A sailing ship, entering Kingston harbour,' he said, pointing. 'Date not known, but let's say round about 1670.'

'Captain Morgan?'

Johnny nodded. 'Before he became governor. Still in his wild, buccaneering days.' He sneaked a look at Kieron, the half-frame glasses perched on his nose, saw that his eyes were intent on the moving finger.

'And here,' Johnny continued, gently rotating the bowl,

'seamen, loading stores, others scouring the drinking dens for a crew....'

'Preparing to embark on his most famous exploit,' Kieron breathed.

'Right,' Johnny said.

'So ...' Kieron said, grasping Johnny's hand and impatiently turning the bowl, 'this next is a violent tropical storm, the vessel sailing due south, and then this last....'

'The last one pretty clear, right Kieron?'

Kieron straightened, his face alight. 'The sacking of Panama.'

'In a nutshell,' Johnny said, grinning.

'Marvellous,' said Kieron Pritchard. 'It's clear as a bell, Johnny, but....'

'But nothing,' said Johnny. 'That's it, there is no more.' He carefully placed the bowl on the stone balustrade, and rubbed his palms together. 'Absolutely the end of story.' He shrugged apologetically.

Kieron frowned. He removed his glasses, tapped the bowl with the plastic tip of one of the slender bows. 'You've told a clear story, in wonderful pictures, Johnny. An absorbing story – but it's not finished. We all know what happened to Henry Morgan, how he sacked Panama, sailed north again, got his knighthood – but there should be more....'

His words trailed away. And as sudden, dawning comprehension lit up his face, he struck his forehead with his palm then shook his head in sheer delight. 'A classic cliffhanger,' he said, and he spread his arms wide. 'Johnny, you've created a nail-biting cliffhanger in exquisite pictures – and if I'm to know the continuation of this story....'

'Then, man, you'd better get yourself one more brass bowl,' Johnny said, smiling broadly as Kieron clapped him on the shoulder and roared with delighted laughter.

They turned as a whisper of sound announced the return of Melody with yet another trolley, this time loaded with plates, serving dishes with silver covers, serviettes in silver rings, and another bottle, misted with condensation, in a bucket in which ice glittered.

And behind her danced Jacko the Lizard, champagne flutes sprouting from between his fingers like the petals of delicate flowers.

'I'm truly humbled, Melody,' Kieron said, moving to the trolley and helping his dark-haired daughter guide it between the rattan chairs. 'All my life I've considered words to be the one perfect medium for transferring thoughts from one person to another. Yet with the greatest ecoomy, your Johnny Lomax has created an enthralling story in delicate line drawings – and they work the same magic as the best of my books.'

'It's just a simple craft, Kieron,' Johnny protested, while all the while through his disbelieving mind ran those incredible words, *your Johnny, your Johnny*....

'Yes, and by comparison mine is an overly complicated process,' Kieron pointed out. 'It certainly achieves the same result, but in this television age what I produce is actually read by scarcely ten per cent of the population.'

Talking animatedly, he was already tucking a napkin into his collar and with his strong white teeth was tearing succulent pieces from a spiced chicken leg.

'Incidentally, this man of yours,' he mumbled to Melody, 'is already trying to sell me another brass bowl. I'd suggest that as my son-in-law, he reduce the price drastically, eh?' A broad smile liberally coated in spicy sauce lit up his face, and as Melody ran to him and kissed his cheek he looked past her, and winked at Johnny.

Johnny helped himself to a plate of chicken, and he watched contentedly as Melody linked arms with her daddy, fondly wiped his mouth with tissue, and wandered with him to the edge of the terrace. Every so often as they chatted her dark head bobbed in that charming way, and once Kieron laughed softly, throwing his head back in delight at something she said.

Oh, man, it's all working out to perfection, Johnny thought – but as he glanced across at the diminutive figure of Jacko the Lizard, dark eyes flashing white as he perched happily on the stone balustrade, he knew there was still the vital question of his methods.

Methods that Solomon Penn had suggested were akin to a shameless confidence trick....

Suddenly, fat spots of warm rain made dark blobs on the

slick marble, and Johnny's stomach turned over. Was this a bad omen, he wondered. A sign that – what was it now? Something another scribe in another place had said, long ago, about the best laid plans of mice and men bein' liable to take a massive nosedive....

Shivering slightly, Johnny signalled to Jacko the Lizard, whispered into his ear, saw the grin light up the thin face, watched him scamper away.

Nervously, he cleared his throat. 'I hate to spoil the party, Kieron, but somewhere floating around there's a letter,' Johnny said, 'which in all honesty must be considered one heck of a blunder –'

'Forget it,' Kieron said, popping the champagne and holding the foaming bottle high. 'Come on, Johnny, fill your glass so that we can drink the best toast I'll ever propose.'

'Yeah, it's one thing to say forget it,' Johnny persisted, feeling like a man feebly treading water, 'but what I'm saying is the perpetrator of any confidence trick deserves to be punished –'

'And, of course, you're right,' Kieron said. Aware now of the increasingly heavy rain, he glanced up at the dark, swollen clouds that had already obscured the moon, then shrugged. 'But I've been wrong before, Johnny, and each mistake has served only to broaden my back. I stand before you, a chastened man.'

'You? Stand before me?' Johnny said weakly, now convinced that he was drowning in a sea of misunderstanding.

'In penance,' Kieron said, sloshing champagne into Johnny's glass. 'I devised a plan to drag you – with some help from Jacko – before my trusted friend and literary peer, Solomon Penn. The idea was to get some shrewd judgement of your worth. In return for parading you in front of him, I expected a long and somewhat rambling letter. But in no more than six short sentences, old Sol gave you his blessing – then took six more to tear me off a strip. Told me I'd wasted valuable time sending a good man for scrutiny, when he could have spent it snoozing in the sun.'

'Oh, Daddy,' Melody said reprovingly. She had moved to Johnny's side, and with the tips of her fingers she touched his cheek, already wet with rain. 'I told you everything about Johnny, so many times, but you just wouldn't listen. You should have trusted my choice, and your own judgement.'

'Mine too, man,' Jacko the Lizard said, skipping from the interior of the now gloomy house, his arms ostentatiously thrust behind his back. 'Didn't I tell you Johnny the Engraver is my big-time friend, always ready with the stickiest sweets and the coolest water – and therefore a damn fine man?'

'Enough,' Kieron said, wiping his hands on a serviette and looking – for the first time – distinctly embarrassed. He picked up his glass, waited for Melody and Johnny to do likewise, then cleared his throat.

'Solomon Penn wrote it down in black and white. Jacko the Lizard's been telling me for weeks. And if I'd had the sense to look, I'd have seen it shining in my own daughter's eyes.' He smiled ruefully. 'Instead, it took a hunk of brass transformed by a clever man into a work of art ...' he lifted his glass to Johnny, dipped his head in acknowledgement, '... to tell me in a roundabout way that I'm a bigoted fool.' He shrugged, his eyes searching their faces. 'So now, I'd like to propose a toast,' he said shakily, and emotion had softened his face, brought a sudden huskiness to his voice. 'To my daughter, Melody – and to her husband-to-be, Johnny Lomax.'

'Ayah,' murmured Jacko the Lizard, bobbing his head approvingly. 'To Johnny the Not-So-Stupid – absodefilutely!'

And with a flourish he whipped his hands from behind his back, snapped the catch of the umbrella he had brought from the carrier of Johnny's bike, and the bright canopy – ragged, misshapen, but nevertheless effective – burst forth like a tropical flower to shelter Johnny and Melody from the now torrential rain.

In this final look at *Caribbean Cool* there are several story writing techniques which, I believe, are worthy of study. It's my particular way of writing, of course, and inevitably (and no matter how much or how little writing experience you have) you will feel that you could perhaps have achieved the effects I was aiming for in a different, or better, way.

But notice how the setting for this final scene – and a brief description of Kieron Pritchard (whom we have not met before) – are given in one paragraph within the opening flashback:

> And when she led him onto a marble terrace of breathtaking beauty, across whose ornamental stone balustrades were visible lush gardens ablaze with bougainvillaea, graceful palms and, beyond, the limpid waters of the Caribbean which the light of the setting sun had turned a soft, flamingo pink, he had managed to meet Kieron Pritchard – cool hands, a hint of expensive aftershave, dark eyes that were not hostile – without betraying for a single moment the turmoil that was threatening to bring him to his knees.

A few paragraphs later a little more is added to that description, and the story is moved neatly forward as Johnny thinks about the letter ...

> In his lightweight linen suit he cut an elegant figure without an ounce of fat in sight. There might even, Johnny dared to hope, be a spark of humanity within him which had been fanned into glorious life by the letter written on the Kingston sands ...

... and all of that description is given through the eyes of the viewpoint character, Johnny Lomax. In fact almost every one of the first 600 words of this final scene are Johnny's thoughts (introspection), as we follow his bicycle trek across town, his passage through the splendid rooms of Kieron Pritchard's house, his consternation at finding Jacko the Lizard there, and his attempts to analyse or comprehend a situation that was totally unexpected.

Of course, there is the overall emotional reversal within the scene that I have suggested is always necessary, but as the scene progresses there are several changes of mood. Johnny feels that everything is going unbelievably well, and he is perhaps naive enough to think that Kieron Pritchard is treating him as a genuine equal because he truly believes that Johnny's engraving skills are no less worthy than his own literary talents.

> He turned to Johnny and again leaned forward, elbows on the knees of his sharply-creased trousers, the brass bowl cupped in one palm. 'What I am saying to you, Johnny – and with much respect – is that I'm not only totally impressed with the skill of your workmanship, but I'm astounded by your obvious profound knowledge of Jamaican history.'
> Johnny felt dazed. He sipped his drink, listened to the distant rattle of the drinks trolley as Jacko the Lizard wheeled it away, was vaguely aware of Kieron Pritchard talking softly to Melody, and then, somehow, he lost the thread ...

At that point Johnny believes everything is going his way, and his euphoria steadily increases until that wonderful moment when he hears:

> ... your Johnny Lomax has created an enthralling story in delicate line drawings – and they work the same magic as the best of my books.'
> 'It's just a simple craft, Kieron,' Johnny protested, while all the while through his disbelieving mind ran those incredible words, *your Johnny, your Johnny....*

But all of this is a little early; Johnny feels that he is counting chickens, the story is proceeding in much too straightforward a manner – and surely there must be an unexpected denouement somewhere....

And, of course, there is.

The ending of *Caribbean Cool* illustrates a technique that always proves very effective. Actually it's a variation of a technique that's sometimes known as the 'gimmick' ending: something that contributes to a story's original conflict is also instrumental in bringing about a satisfactory conclusion. I used that technique in its purest form in a story called *A Scream in the Night*. A man and woman driving a Landrover out of Kabul collided with a camel and were caught by pursuing tribesmen. Later, after much excitement, they fled, and were able to make their escape on, yes, that poor battered camel.

Here, the umbrella was mentioned in Johnny's first meeting with Melody. It didn't add one jot to the conflict, but it proved effective then in sheltering the couple from the rain, and it proves just as effective later as a colourful, unusual, but apposite close to the story.

Now. Did you decide where the ending began?

As you know by now, I believe that a story has a natural beginning, middle and end without, as Eric Morecambe might have said, any visible join. But if I had to choose the moment in *Caribbean Cool* when the end game begins, then it must be when Johnny Lomax whispers to Jacko the Lizard (sending him for the umbrella), and nervously clears his throat.

Because it's here that Johnny raises the question of the letter, which was his last-ditch attempt to secure the hand of the delectable Melody. Kieron opens his heart, and in the denouement reveals that what Johnny had thought to be his own carefully planned operation had been fixed from the start, and the story moves smoothly to a satisfying conclusion.

SUMMARY

Where did the idea come from?

That question always intrigues me when I ask it of myself, for often I haven't a clue. One story I wrote began with the vague idea of an old man in northern Queensland who had a small shop and was concerned about the influx of Japanese settlers. When written, he was a retired mechanic who did repairs in his spare time and had recently hired a stranger to help out.

Caribbean Cool began with a character, Rajah Penn, who was originally conceived by my wife, Patricia, as an Indian detective who arrives in England and is first seen standing in a railway station. Later he became a writer of letters in a crowded Indian office, then I took over and, well, you've read the result.

I took something like twenty to twenty-four hours to write the story – three full working days – and I had no idea where I was going to send it. That, you will say, goes against every bit of advice you've ever read, while as far as I'm concerned it's completely in accord with the best advice you're ever likely to get: before you write for anyone else, write for yourself.

9   Afterthoughts

There is a stage reached when, with a feeling of ineffable delight, we have before us a complete short story. But however pleasing the moment may be, it is brief. Much has gone before, and there is still much to do before those ten pages or so are ready to be sent out for an editor's consideration.

For me this progression from the original idea to the completed manuscript almost always follows the same pattern. A lot of it is going on in the mind when to others I appear to be washing the car, or reading. It's only when they notice that I've spent half an hour polishing the same wing or haven't turned a page – or blinked – in a long while that they realize all is not as it seems. If it's my wife, she'll merely raise one eyebrow and say, 'Working, John?' and I'll mumble something unintelligible and splatter more Turtle Wax on the already glistening paintwork, or flick back a dozen pages until I reach a bit I remember.

In this chapter we'll take a quick glance over our shoulder at what's been done: those hours of thinking and dreaming and gazing at a flickering screen (or sheet of paper) leading up to that indescribable moment when the story – however rough – is there in black and white (or green and black); and then we'll look ahead to the shaping and polishing that must be done to any story before it can, with confidence, be slipped into its manila envelope.

We will cover:

- Gestation
- Revision
- Titles
- The editorial scissors
- Persistence
- Presentation

Gestation

Under this heading I am considering conception to be the first glimmer of an idea – the first twinkle in your mind's eye – and birth to be the moment when you sit down and write the first word of the first sentence of your story. The birth can be difficult; indeed, very few short stories are produced without a deal of hard labour; but I am one of those writers who believe that if the gestation period is nourished with creative thought and allowed to run its course, then the birth pains will be eased. More importantly, the offspring will stand a better chance of survival in what is, without doubt, a cut-throat and increasingly competitive market.

Hark back if you will to my recent musings on the way an idea can change out of all recognition. The Indian detective Rajah Penn became Solomon Penn, a writer of letters on a sun-kissed Kingston beach. The change came about partly through letting that hazy figure drift about in my mind as I went about other things, and partly through sitting down at my word processor and keying words into a blank PLOTSKEL.

From a writer of letters who himself was an interesting character I progressed to somebody who would need his services, and with the arrival on the scene of Johnny Lomax I had my main character. Rajah/Solomon Penn had undergone another change: he was now destined to play a supporting role.

You will find this happening constantly as you go about your business of dreaming up stories, and you must actively – or passively – encourage that happening without ever losing sight of those guiding principles: there must be conflict, that conflict must be of vital importance to your main character, and the consequences of failure must be disastrous.

I find it best to work this way.

At any one time there are usually two or three characters about whom I intend to write a story. Two will be vague images floating around on the surface of my subconscious, occasionally sticking a hand or a leg up to grab my attention so that for a while I concentrate, and learn a little more about them. Then, ruthlessly, I let them sink once more into the murky depths while I get on with more important things.

The third character will have completed that process. I will have a clear image in my conscious mind, and I will know some of the story – though possibly not the ending. And it's now that I sit down at my desk and create a full story outline by entering the events in chronological order on a blank PLOTSKEL.

Even now the ending may not come to me. For although I said the first word of the first sentence is the moment of birth, there is an overlap; the gestation process continues well into the actual writing. What appears to happen is that the subconscious plays about with notions as yet unrevealed, watches and takes furtive notes as I write, ducks beneath the surface to do some quick calculations on what can only be an electronic plot analyser – then rises like Flipper to toss the perfect resolution to the story in my lap.

And it really does come as mysteriously as that.

Revision

If gestation in short story terms is cerebral, then revision is definitely sweat-of-the-brow.

Paradoxically, however, you should begin it by doing nothing.

Somehow you must distance yourself from a story that has been in your thoughts for weeks, possibly months, and the only way to do that is to put it away in a drawer and forget about it. Even twenty-four hours can see details begin to fade, but I would recommend much longer than that because your subconscious doesn't yet want to give up; like a fire's dying embers it will flare into life and spit alternatives and suggestions which, if acted upon, could have you rushing to alter a story that is already perfect – but you cannot know that, yet, because you are still too close.

In a week, or a fortnight, with two fresh characters swimming about in vaguely conceived situations and a third already fighting its way through a tangled PLOTSKEL, take out your completed story and read it as a stranger. Don't start altering after the first paragraph. Sit down without pen or pencil and force yourself to read from beginning to end – then read it again. Only then think about making notes, and initially do this by underlining words or phrases, and jotting pertinent comments in the margin.

What you are hoping to grasp in that first reading is the overall feeling of the complete story. Do you *like* the story? Do you get a feeling of pleasure as you read it? Disregarding the faults that you are certain to notice, is the general impression that of a piece of work indistinguishable from those you would expect to see in a modern glossy magazine – and I give you that point of reference as a rough guide only, for although you are aiming for that professional standard, you are also hoping to go one better and produce a refreshingly original story. Is the beginning interesting? Does the story move forward, with every word your characters utter having some relevance to the plot? Does the ending leave you feeling satisfied, perhaps wishing there was a little more – because most good stories do that – but knowing in your heart that if it had gone on for just another paragraph, it could have been ruined?

If all seems well, then you can begin to revise.

You may well find that some sections of the story are in the wrong place. A paragraph of descriptive prose may be more effective coming earlier, or later, the tension increased if a character makes a pointed statement at a different time.

Remember that a word is emphasized if it comes at the beginning or the end of a sentence. *His fist slammed against Mason's jaw* can be rewritten as *he slammed Mason's jaw with his fist*, and in sentences like that you must decide which version is the one that creates the desired effect.

Look for the big faults first, then move in closer and look at the fine detail. Literals (typing errors) are often difficult to spot, as our eyes seem to slide over them. A computer spell check program is a great help, but if you are still using a typewriter, then again it's a matter of hard slogging. Continuity is not so important as it is in a novel, but even in these shorter works you will find that half-way through your story blue eyes have turned brown, jeans have become cords, and the girl you called Marge is now Madge.

Some people have a crib sheet they refer to, listing things like repetition, clarity, dialogue, and so on. With experience as my guide I tend simply to read each paragraph word by word, taking my time, concentrating, and seeing if there is anything there that jars, or if there is any way I can improve what I have written.

Done this way you will spot repetition without conscious thought; the same words coming too close together will leap off the page. Too many alternatives for *he said* will have the same effect; they are always more intrusive and irritating than the words they replace. You will notice sentences that are unclear, dialogue that sounds stiff, action scenes that are over too quickly and conversations that drag on for too long.

Try to make your verbs stand alone. It's much better to say 'he plodded' than 'he walked slowly'.

Always seek exactly the right word to express what you are trying to say, but if the choice is between an obscure long word or a familiar short one, use the short one every time.

I also mentioned that I look for any way that I can improve what I have written. Rewriting sentences to alter the emphasis is part of it, and this is something that really does get easier as you gain experience. But even as a beginner you will see whole chunks of your story that you know you can make more pleasing to the eye, and to the mind's ear: that important critical faculty that is actually listening to the words as the eye passes over them.

Finally in this section on revision, I must make brief mention of clichés. If the definition of a cliché is a phrase that was once original but is now so over-used that it has become an irritant, then the rapid expansion of television coverage of everything from political rallies to the Oscar ceremonies produces new ones every week.

Modern examples include *take on board, very much so,* and *at the end of the day*, while *sick as a parrot, fit as a fiddle, fresh as a daisy*, and *the life and soul of the party* have all been around for years.

I'd make an absolute rule here and say never use them in any of your stories unless they issue from the mouths of your characters. Even then, use them sparingly. People do use clichés in their speech; they spring quickly to mind and are understood by the masses which, presumably, is why so many politicians say *at the end of the day* rather than *ultimately*. But if you go too far and have your characters talking in clichés every time they open their mouths, then far from bringing them realistically to life, you will create parodies of real people, and that's not the effect you want.

LAYOUT

The layout of your story is important not only in the way that it appears on your A4 page, but in the way it is likely to appear in a certain publication. In simple terms, paragraphs are blocks of related information, and when the subject changes, then so does the paragraph. The trouble is, if you are writing away and your information blocks are all the same size, then your paragraphs are going to look too uniform – all too large, or all too small.

This is further complicated when you consider your target publication's printed page. At the two extremes you will have a literary magazine that uses small print right across a large page, and a newspaper that splits its page into narrow columns – making your paragraphs look too small in the one, or much too large in the other.

Ideally, you must aim for a layout that is never repetitious or monotonous, and you can do that by varying the length of your sentences and the size of your paragraphs.

A one line paragraph is fine for emphasis.

But don't have too many.

Titles

This is one of several subjects over which many writers tear their hair (the other is the editorial scissors, of which more later). The reason is that although we are told that a good title can sell a story and so we must take great care to choose the best we can, having done that, we frequently find that the fiction editor will substitute one that – to us – is unquestionably inferior.

A case in point is one story I sold to a women's magazine. It was about two little boys who were out in the woods looking for gold because mum's birthday was approaching and they needed a present. Now, when I wrote the story in 1970 I'd called it *The Fossickers*, and in 1993 (yes, it took that long to sell) I still thought the title was pretty good. But when it appeared in the magazine it had been changed to *A Present For Mum*.

Was I pleased? No. Did I do anything about it? No. Because this is something you will learn to accept – and anyway, there was the story, in print, and I should have been satisfied. Ah, but was I? Well, since you ask, yes and no. Because, as you will see, the editorial scissors had also been at work.

Often, a title chooses itself. A line or phrase within the story stands out, and when used as the title seems to capture the essence of the tale in just four or five words. A story I sold to the *Alfred Hitchcock Mystery Magazine* was about a man who had been wronged four times by another, and when that man stole his girl the victim went after him. The story was called *Fifth Time Dead*, and in the first draft that was the final line of the story: *I made my way back to Craignure to finish the business I had with Dougail Gaunt, four times lucky but fifth time dead*. It was changed (by me) for the published version, but I kept the title.

That's an example of a line taken from a story and used as the title, and another chosen in the same way was *The Last Thing on Her Mind*, which was actually part of a line of dialogue. I've already mentioned *The Fossickers*, which is simply two words that tell readers – in colloquial Australian – that someone in the story is *rummaging for gold in cracks or crevices*. Another is *Binky and Sam and the Travelling Man*, which is self-explanatory.

That one is also an example of an editorial change. It was printed under that title in *The Australian Women's Weekly*, but *Woman and Home* changed it to *Tale of a Travelling Man*. You will probably have your own preference, but I like the original.

You can use well known sayings, snatches of quotations or lines of verse that seem apt; one of my stories (still unsold) is called *And He Sang to a Small Guitar*, another *A Toe on the Ladder*, while yet another was entitled *All the Colours of the Rainbow*.

The Editorial Scissors

I must admit, now, that in 99% of my writing I have had no cause to complain about alterations done by well-meaning editors. Where it has occurred it has usually been in newspaper feature writing of which I do an enormous amount, where if a piece is too long editors tend to cut from the bottom up – regardless of content – which is why in newspaper writing you try to put all your important information near the beginning. (Digressing again!)

But in *The Fossickers* – or *A Present For Mum* – a bit of information was left out that was vitally important. Near the beginning of the story the two little boys were frightened by a loud yell, and ran deep into the woods. But for some reason the sentence in which the yell featured was excised by the editor. Later, one boy asked the other why they ran, and he was told it was *because that big yell scared you out of your socks* – but of course all mention of it had been deleted, which meant observant readers would have been mystified.

You will find your work being cut if a 3,000-word piece has been accepted when 2,500 words were required. But don't bank on that happening; wrong length usually means rejection. Instead, you can expect minor alterations to grammar, punctuation, for clarification, to cut out unacceptable words (in one of my stories 'bushman' was substituted for 'Abo'), and if you are selling overseas, the odd colloquialism introduced for authenticity.

What all that means, of course, is that the editorial scissors are just as likely to be the editorial pen, and frequently your stories are edited with great care, and are the better for it.

There's not a lot I can say about political correctness, because my own feeling is that in fiction it should be possible to say anything. No space here, either, to discuss the Salman Rushdie affair, but my own feelings on that are as strong as those of any writer of fiction.

But if you are hoping to sell your stories to magazines, then you must have a good idea of what is acceptable. You can do your own research by reading published stories in your target magazines and seeing if people swear (and if so how coarsely), smoke, drink, and – as used to be in the case in films – keep one foot on the floor when they are in bed with a member (oops!) of the opposite sex.

Another ideal way of finding out just what you can include in your stories is to send away for editorial guidelines. In 1990, the American magazine, *Good Housekeeping*, said that:

... they look for stories of emotional interest to women –

courtship, romance, marriage, family, friendship, personal growth, coming of age. They prefer manuscripts to be typewritten, double-spaced, between 1,000 and 3,000 words and accompanied by a short cover letter listing previous writing credits.

In this country, *Woman's Weekly* says:

Stories should be between 1,000 and 5,000 words. Short stories can be on any theme, but must have love as the central core of the plot, whether in a specific romantic context, within the family, or mankind in general. Stories should present a positive attitude to life.

There should be no explicit sex. No sex outside marriage. We avoid political or racial plots and stories with violent backgrounds; science fiction; the occult. Plots should not be based on class conflict. Characters do not smoke. They can drink in moderation, but never drink and drive.

Persistence

Taking for granted that there exists a modicum of talent, persistence is the one quality above all others that will bring you success. But even that persistence must not be blind, or misguided.

I began writing in 1959 when I was a young soldier of 23. I sold a story very quickly (a short piece to *Soldier Magazine*), won army short story competitions, and over a three-year period wrote regular monthly stories for a squadron magazine in Gibraltar. No pay, but invaluable experience. I didn't manage another sale to a national magazine until 1970 – some ten years after the first.

But I never stopped trying.

That second important sale was in Australia, and subsequently during the five years I lived there I sold poetry, thriller short stories to a pulp magazine, and more stories to national women's weekly and monthly magazines. I returned to England in 1974 and – yes, that's right – sales dried up and I think I sold just three or four stories in the next fifteen years.

The comparison with my previous success is a little unfair, because during those later years I was involved with starting and running a business. Once I returned to writing it was with great dedication, and by 1989 I was a full-time writer, with a reasonable income coming from newspaper journalism, article writing, short stories and books.

I make no apology for giving you that potted life story. I began it because I wanted to paint a clear picture of success coming through persistence – stickability, if you like – without in any way suggesting that I have any great talent. But when I look back on what I have written, I realize that there is evident – to me, at least – one driving force that above all others was the reason for that persistence: what I was always seeking was fame, not fortune.

No, not fame, Recognition.

If you are a writer, you begin writing not because you want to make money, but because you want to write. When you send stories away you are hoping to receive a cheque, certainly; but much more than that you are seeking recognition; you are hoping desperately that somebody out there is going to say, yes, that story is good enough to be published in a magazine that is going to be read by thousands, possibly millions of people.

When that time comes, the cheque isn't important. But the sight of your work in print, in a glossy magazine, is intoxicating. It came to me in Australia. My wife and I were in tears.

If you are a writer, you will write. They say that running is addictive, and I say that if you are a writer then writing is a compulsion, and you persist with it because you are striving for perfection but will carry on anyway because you are besotted with words and the way they can be combined to form something that, in the end, has a beauty that enchants you, and always will.

And so I come back to the one theme that I hope runs like

a thread of pure gold through this simple book: when you are seeking perfection, it must be perfection as seen, judged, appreciated, by your eyes. And if you do persist, always, I guarantee that you will find the success of publication when – in your eyes – you are a long way from that perfection.

For you must always be your own, sternest critic.

Presentation

Right, let's come back to earth.

If perfection is hard to achieve in your writing, in your presentation it must come as second nature. By presentation I mean the look of your manuscript when a busy editor tears open the envelope and lets it slide onto the desk.

My own work goes out on A4 paper, double spaced, with a two-inch margin on the left and one of a reasonable size on the right. I leave the right-hand edge of the typescript jagged (not justified, which would look like a page from this book). Page numbers appear top right. MF (more follows) goes bottom right.

As a point of interest though not of concern, the United States equivalent paper size is 8.5 x 11 inches. But stories I have sold there have all been presented on A4.

I put a title page at the front of every manuscript. This has my name and address top right, the title of the story centred just above halfway down the page, 'by' centred beneath that, then my name, also centred. The approximate word count comes next. Near the bottom I put 'First British Serial Rights'.

For a long time I thought that this was a complete waste of time. Then I sold a story to a UK magazine (not the first one they'd taken), and when the cheque came back it was attached to their usual editorial contribution docket on which were typed the rights they were buying. The back of the cheque had a space for the author's signature. I knew I could not pay the cheque into my account unless I signed the back, and my signature would mean that I was agreeing to sell the rights named.

Unfortunately, this time they had typed 'All Rights'.

The problem was soon sorted out, and I'm merely relating this incident to let you know that it's always advisable to put those four words – or the initials FBSR – at the bottom of your title page, and to ensure when you do get an acceptance that *you are selling only those rights*.

What FBSR means is that the publication you sell to has the right to reproduce the material and publish it for the first time in the United Kingdom, and once only. Once published, you can then sell second, third and subsequent British serial rights, and the first rights to other countries – First North American, First Australasian, and so on.

If I had agreed to sell All Rights, that would have been the end of it, and the story I had spent many hours on would no longer have been mine.

It's also a good idea to put a blank sheet of paper after the last page. This makes matters easier when your story has been rejected; for freshness when resubmitting you should retype the title page but at the end of the MS you need only replace the blank sheet.

The method of preparing a manuscript for presentation to the American market is much different. A title page is not used. Your name and address go in the top left corner, the word count in the top right. The title is centred approximately one-third of the way down the page, put your byline (the name you are writing under – your own, or a pseudonym) beneath that, and after dropping down two double spaces, begin your story.

There is never any need to put a covering letter in with your story. Well, almost never. There will come a time when you are sending out a story that has already been published. In those cases it's always best to inform the editor where and when the story previously appeared. Also, particularly when selling to the USA, you will find it helpful to mention any successes you may have had.

The only other occasion that immediately springs to mind

is if you are submitting a seasonal story. This will need to go out several months in advance, so the editor will need to know that it is, say, a story intended for Christmas.

10   Conclusions

Summing Up

It's one thing to set out to produce a book entitled *Practical Short Story Writing*, but to arrange the contents in an order that enables a reader to use them in a practical way takes a great deal of thought, and planning. Or is that being presumptuous? After all, in the beginning there is always the idea which is then developed into a story in which various devices are employed to hold the reader's attention, and after two or three thousand words the story ends, leaving the reader with a feeling of satisfaction.

That's the ideal towards which we all aim. And looking back over the previous nine chapters I feel that to help you reach that end they have presented a vast amount of practical information in a way that will be understood by raw beginners, and appreciated by those writers who have reached some competence but find regular publication eluding them.

My own feeling is that Chapters 2 to 5 are the core of the book, offering valuable practical instruction that may be new – and enlightening – to many readers. I believe it's to these chapters that readers will turn, using them as handy reference when – during the course of their writing – they become bogged down or uncertain about how to employ traditional storytelling techniques.

But technique on its own is of no use at all. So Chapter 6 offers some advice on the important organization that will ease the transition from vague mental images to the mass of words on paper that constitute a short story; organization that involves time, a place to work, and the writing wherewithal.

Even when the story is written, the work is not finished. It's then that a writer must contrive to step back from the finished story and somehow view it through the eyes of a reader who has flicked through a magazine, stopped at the fiction page, and lingered there just long enough to see if there's anything worth reading. So in Chapter 9 we not only discuss gestation, but also mention that revision begins with that period when writers distance themselves from their work so that – after a day, a week, or a month – they return to it with their minds refreshed, and are in turn both enchanted and appalled by what they have written.

If I've done my job, then *Practical Short Story Writing* is one way for you to learn something of the complicated techniques needed to take a story from the idea stage to the glossy pages of a magazine – and I say that in the painful knowledge that those techniques come naturally to gifted writers.

But there are other ways.

Over the years there have been many correspondence courses – I believe it's now called 'distance learning' – on all kinds of writing, some of them by schools that teach nothing but journalism, others by schools that have many writing departments, and still others that teach everything from engineering to flower-arranging and have a creative writing department listed in their prospectus.

Are they any good? On the whole, yes, they are very good. Some provide several hardback books by well-known authors, and professionally printed lessons in useful binders. Most have tutors who are full-time writers able to pass on a great deal of knowledge that has taken them years to acquire. Often several years are allowed to complete a course. Some schools offer money-back guarantees, usually you can pay by instalments, and many provide certificates (which are of no use if you are a writer of fiction, and of doubtful worth even if you specialize in journalism or some other form of writing).

In Chapter 6 I talked about organization, and if it does nothing else a correspondence course will give you a planned study programme and an additional incentive to do some writing every day. And because the interchange of information is all done in writing, then virtually everything you do on the course will be valuable practice of one kind or another.

Creative writing classes are far less prevalent in the UK than they are on the other side of the Atlantic, although many schools and colleges often hold evening or day classes – mainly during the winter months. I believe that creative writing is itself a somewhat misleading term; unless you are copying something already written, everything you write must be creative. I know what the term is supposed to mean: the production of written work – usually fiction – that is entirely original; but again we hit a paradox, because how can originality be taught?

My own opinion is that, as with correspondence courses, a lot of the value of creative writing classes is in the organization they give to your writing time. But because I have never in my life attended a creative writing class I realize that with ignorant criticism I am probably doing those who run them a disservice. At the very least you will be among people with similar interests, and informal chat during coffee breaks – when the instructor joins in and answers questions – can be as valuable as the actual lessons.

A Short Story Check List

During this book I have stressed the need always to write not for money, nor for some unknown editor – but for yourself. And reading through a story after letting it gather some dust in a bottom drawer will to some extent show you if the story that was so wondrously clear in your mind has retained its magic as you used pen, typewriter or computer to record it on the blank page.

But because you are reading work with which you are inevitably still too familiar, and because the eye that is used to reading tends always to see what it thinks is written rather than what is actually on the printed page, it does help if you have a few pointers to guide you in your critical assessment.

There is nothing new about a list that you can use to check the structure, content and effect of a finished story. Indeed, once you have gained experience you will probably have your own set of guidelines that you use as you go about your revision – even if they are simply triggers in your subconscious that set alarm bells ringing each time you come across something that's glaringly out of kilter.

The check list I use is an amalgam of those finer points that over the years I have discovered to be essential to any short story's success. But, as I've done so many times before, I will qualify that statement: when I talk about success, I mean that the story has succeeded *for me*; has succeeded to *my satisfaction*, and not in a way I think may please an editor who is going to be reading it subjectively.

It goes something like this:

1   PRESENTATION
    I'm going to start with last things first, working on the assumption that unless you or an editor can actually read the story, the contents might just as well be garbage. So check your presentation. Have you got the correct front page for the market – UK or USA – with your name and address, title, pseudonym if any, number of words and rights offered all absolutely clear and correct? Are your pages numbered? Is the text double-spaced and typed or printed with a new, black ribbon? It's sometimes advisable to put MF at the bottom of each page except the last, which should instead have END (and, if you wish, your name followed by the copyright symbol).

2   HAS THE STORY STARTED IN THE RIGHT PLACE?
    In Chapter 4, we discovered that to capture the reader's attention a short story must begin at a dramatic high point. It

was suggested that the REACTION stage of your PLOTSKEL usually constitutes such a point. My own experience has taught me that it is rare for a writer to start too far into a story, but quite common to start too soon. So one good way of checking if you have started at exactly the right place is to see if dispensing with one or more of the opening paragraphs gives your story more impact: can you start a little later in the story, and give the information contained in those first paragraphs in a later flashback?

3 IS THE CONFLICT STRONG ENOUGH?

This doesn't mean that the heroine must be tied to a log floating down a crocodile-infested river while the hero frantically attempts to rescue her before the log tumbles into the foaming rapids. What it does mean is that the problem faced by your main character must be of vital importance, and the consequences of failure to resolve that problem disastrous – in the given circumstances. In other words, a young woman hoping for a university degree so that she can become a doctor is forced to give up her studies because her widowed mother becomes ill; not a life-threatening problem for the girl, but certainly one that can see her ambitions thwarted, if not destroyed.

4 HAVE YOU CHOSEN THE RIGHT VIEWPOINT?

This one is not so straightforward. Certainly the obvious choice is to tell the story through the actions and emotions of the person with the problem, because empathy is probably the most important factor that will draw a reader into your story. But because of the restrictions of viewpoint – what you reveal can only be those events seen, heard or experienced by your viewpoint character – it is sometimes more advantageous to tell the story through a minor character who is able to describe events that happen 'off screen', while still maintaining the high drama of close involvement.

5 HAVE YOU GOT THE FIVE ESSENTIALS IN EARLY?

Not only must you start your story in the right place, you must involve your reader with an interesting character who has a fight on his hands, place that character in an attractive, exotic or intriguing setting, create a suitable and easily identifiable mood, and introduce a *hook* that compels your reader to read on. You must do all of this within the first couple of pages – and if you haven't, then go back and rewrite until you have.

6   ARE YOUR FLASHBACKS CONFUSING?
Never move into a flashback sequence until you have successfully established those five essentials. Your readers must recognize and be sympathetic with your main character – and know something of the problem – before you take that tricky step back in time to describe previous events. And the moment you take that backward step must be instantly recognizable, the return to the present smoothly accomplished.

7   HAVE YOU MADE USE OF THE FIVE SENSES?
Gravel crunches underfoot. The scent of new-mown grass in spring is unmistakable. A biting east wind can be agony to the ears, the sound of a Beethoven symphony exquisite pleasure, the first bite of a sloe sharp enough to parch the mouth. Your characters experience with their eyes, their ears, their sense of smell, touch and taste, and these sensations experienced vicariously by your readers will heighten their enjoyment of your story.

8   DOES YOUR DIALOGUE FLOW NATURALLY?
There's an important qualification here, too, for your dialogue must only give the *illusion* of flowing naturally. Many teachers suggest reading your dialogue aloud, and this certainly helps in some ways – you discover at once that your character would be gasping for breath before getting half-way through his lengthy diatribe. But you must also make sure that everything your characters say has meaning, and moves the story forward – and don't forget that the way they speak is an excellent way of revealing their character.

9   HAVE YOU WRITTEN SCENICALLY?
This may seem to be asking the same question as check number 6, and indeed I am imploring you to paint a vivid

picture. But when I ask if you have written scenically I mean have you, firstly, constructed each scene – either intuitively or deliberately – so that through the emotional reversal within it the reader will want to turn the page to find out what happens next? And secondly, is each scene akin to those *Only Fools and Horses* examples I quoted in Chapter 3, creating not just anticipation but moving your story in space and time – and that, of course, means forward.

10 IS YOUR ENDING SATISFYING?
Endings are funny things. You can't rush them, you can't let them drag on interminably. And what on earth do we mean by 'satisfying'? If you read short stories you will know the ones that have left you with a warm feeling, though you may not have bothered to find out why. In this book we discussed *Caribbean Cool* in great detail, and I'd like to leave you with that ending, and the ending of *Binky and Sam and the Travelling Man*. I like them both; and from a letter passed on to me by the publishers I learned that the second was so effective it moved a grandmother in Australia to tears.

First, *Caribbean Cool* ...

And with a flourish he whipped his hands from behind his back, snapped the catch of the umbrella he had brought from the carrier of Johnny's bike, and the bright canopy – ragged, misshapen, but nevertheless effective – burst forth like a tropical flower to shelter Johnny and Melody from the now torrential rain.

and, finally, *Binky and Sam* ...

So this is what it's like, Binky marvelled, listening to his heart. This is what we've been missing, all those long, lonely years. Not that they'd been sad years, or bad years, no, not by a heck of a long piece of chalk. But if the thought of what this could mean – always bearing in mind that nothing's settled till it's settled – has knocked me for a spinner, poor old Sammy's going to think she's backed the winner of the Melbourne Cup and won the Golden Casket all in the one crazy afternoon.

'Did I ever tell you, Col,' he mused, 'that we never did get around to having kids of our own.'

But the dark little man was lost, somewhere in a dream, and tight up against his chest a tiny blond shrimp was staring with unseeing blue eyes at a distant, golden beach.

Useful Addresses

Freelance Press Services
Cumberland House
Lissadel Street
Salford M6 6GG
Tel: 061 745 8850

The Writers' and Artists'
  Year Book
A & C Black
35 Bedford Row
London WC1R 4JH
Tel: 071 242 0946

The Writer's Handbook
Macmillan Press Ltd.
Houndmills, Basingstoke
Hampshire RG21 2XS
Tel: 0256 29242

Writer's Digest Books
F & W Publications
1507 Dana Avenue
Cincinnati
Ohio 45207 USA

Writers' Monthly
29 Turnpike Lane
London N8 0EP
Tel: 081 342 8879

Writers News
PO Box 4
Nairn
Scotland IV12 4HU
Tel: 0667 54441

Index